# Sometimes God Even Cries

## A Teaching Testimonial of God's Love During Times of Difficulty

A novel by
Dana Bach

PublishAmerica
Baltimore

ISBN: 1-4241-6206-8
PUBLISHED BY PUBLISHAMERICA, LLLP
www.publishamerica.com
Baltimore


Printed in the United States of America

# Foreword

This writing is a work of fiction based upon certain elements of fact. Names, characters, places and events are quasi-symbolic of the author's imagination and in general are used fictitiously. Any and all resemblance to any living persons is solely coincidental.

It is the author intent to share with his readers in a first person genre that the path of life cannot be walked alone; regardless of ones belief system—be that of a supreme deity or in the rejection of organized religion beliefs altogether.

Like it or not, accept it or not...*We Never Walk Alone*.

# Table of Contents

# Chapter 1: In the Beginning

"Good morning, class. This morning I'd like to—alright children, now please settle down and take your seats," remarked Abigail Anderson to her third grade Sunday school class, "We have a great deal of scripture to cover this morning before the bells chime for worship." She continued on by saying, "Last week we completed verse twenty-five in the book of Genesis, so today let's move on and discuss verses 26 through 28. Who would like you to help me by beginning to read verse 26?"

"I will, Mrs. Anderson, I will," cried out Clark Norton in an overenthusiastic tone. "I've been practicing my reading all week."

"Very well, Clark—begin reading verse 26, please," said Abigail.

"Verse 26; Then God said, 'Let Us make man in our image, according to Our likeness; let them have dominion over the fish of the sea, over the birds of the air, and over the cattle, over all the earth and over every creeping thing that creeps on the earth.' Should I continue, Mrs. Anderson?"

Abigail nodded her head, giving her approval to continue.

"Verse 27; So God created man in His own image; in the image of God He created him; male and female He created them. Verse 28; Then God blessed them, and God said to them, 'be fruitful and multiply; fill the earth and subdue it; have dominion over the fish of the sea, over the birds of the air, and over every living thing that moves on the earth.'"

"Thank you, Clark, I can see that you have been spending some quality time practicing your reading, you did a very good job," replied Abigail. "Class—there are a couple of words in the three verses that Clark read I think we need to discuss—the first word is 'subdue' and the second word is 'dominion.' Remember in order to interpret what the Bible is telling us we must first understand the meaning of the words used. The word 'subdue' and the word 'dominion' both have similar meanings—to be in charge of and have authority over. What these verses are saying is that it was God's plan for mankind; actually it was Adam & Eve at first, who was to take care of and be responsible for all living things upon the earth.

"How many of you have pets at home? Please don't say anything, class, just raise your hands. Almost all of you, I can see. And do each of you make sure that your pets have food and water? Do you give them a bath when they need it? That's great—that's the way God intended for it to be, for mankind to be in charge of the animals.

"Does anyone have any questions concerning our new words? No—very well, then. Let's go on. Did each of you read these verses before coming to Sunday school this morning, and are you using the Bibles I gave you? Good, I'm proud of you. It's very important that you use the Bible I gave each of you.

"There are many different versions of the Bible. The version I gave you to study out of is called the 'New King James' version, written in, more or less, plain English, making it easier for you to understand, instead of using words they used a long time ago such as 'thee' or 'thou.' I know it can be very confusing. I just want each of you to note that there are times in the Bible, as you read in verse 25, that you will find words capitalized when giving reference to God Himself; words such as 'Us', 'Our', 'He', 'Him.' This is done to show respect for our Lord and Savior. Okay, class, we must move on. Thinking back to the first verse in Genesis, who can tell me in your own words what we have learned so far?" asked Mrs. Anderson.

There was silence within the room for several minutes. Abigail, seeing the overall bewildered look upon her class, opted to give her own explanation so as not to single out any one child particularly, yet before she could, a little voice from the back of the room, barely audible, asked, "Can I try?"

"Yes, you may," answered Abigail, not recognizing the voice. "Please come up front—we can hardly hear you from your seat."

A pretty little blond-haired, freckle-faced girl stood up from her chair, just barely standing above the desktop, approached the front of the class saying, "Hi, my name is Allison—we just moved here and this is my first week in Sunday school. My mother told me I would make new friends if I came to Sunday school, but…no one has talked to me yet. Is it still okay if I try the answer?" asked Allison.

"Allison—we're so glad you came today. I'm Mrs. Anderson and this is the third grade Bible study class. Everyone say hello to Allison."

In unison twelve youngsters, some at the top of their lungs, all greeted Allison with a hearty, "Hello, Allison," but before Abigail could say another word, little Allison began telling her new classmates the story of creation as she understood it.

"In the very beginning God made everything. He made heaven where he lives and the earth where we live. Here on the earth, he made mountains and the oceans and even the deserts. He made all the different animals, but most important—God made, He called it 'Creation', but my mom used the word 'made' when she read the Bible to me when I was little. Anyway—he made men and women in His own image. I think that means we kinda look like Him. Oh yeah, he also made everything we need to live here on the earth, like food and water."

"Allison, that was a good example of what we can learn by reading the first book in the Bible. Don't you agree, class? Thank you so much for sharing your explanation with us," said Abigail, "but before you sit back down; class, we have a few minutes before the bells start to chime. Why don't we each introduce ourselves to our new friend, and then, Allison, you can share with us whatever you would like to say about yourself; where you moved from, what elementary school you will be attending, what area of the city you live in. Sharing is a good way to learn about others and, before you know it, we'll all be good friends."

Little Allison just stood without saying a word, leaning on the corner of the desk, nervously rubbing the tip of her right shoe against the desk leg where she stood.

Once again, it was Clark who came to the rescue, to be the first to speak up, "Hello, Allison. My name is Clark and I am seven years old and live on Ambler Avenue, I go to Weil Elementary School and like everyone else here I am in the third grade."

Before anyone else had a chance to speak, the bells began to toll, signaling there were only twenty minutes before the organist started playing the processional leading into the liturgy. Abigail, having gathered together her teaching supplies and placing them in an overstuffed attaché case, led her class in closing prayer, steering each child to the chapel where they were to locate their families to prepare for church services.

Upon entering the chapel, not seeing me, she found seating for us, as was our usual practice to sit in either the first or second pew from the altar, generally at the end closest to the center aisle. Thinking to herself, she mentally calculated the number of Sundays she and Matthew had sat on the same pew since their marriage; twelve years at an average of fifty services each year. *Wow,* she thought, *that's over six hundred Sundays*, reckoning the only times they had missed a Sunday worship service was generally only once each year when out of town for summer vacation.

When I arrived, I asked Abigail, "How was your class this morning?"

"Actually—enlightening," she responded. "I'm embarrassed to admit this, but I still haven't learned all the names of the children in my class. This morning there was the cutest little girl—blond hair, freckles and big blue eyes—who just stole my heart. I asked for someone to summarize what we had studied so far and her answer was most impressive. Matthew, the sad part is I didn't even know she was in the room until she spoke up. I never saw her sitting in the back row, well—next week I've decided that before my class meets I'll have all their chairs setup in a semicircular pattern to avoid my overlooking any student ever again. Matthew—are you listening to me?"

I nodded my head with a gentle whisper, saying, "Yes, dear, I am."

"Matthew—there's another thing that bothering me, too. Now I know that it shouldn't, but it does; she wasn't dressed like all the other girls—most mother's dress their daughters up a bit for church. I mean her clothes were in disarray, shoes were scuffed and her hair looked as if it hadn't been brushed. Her appearance was just unkempt, as if no one cared about her appearance. If we were to have a daughter I *would never* allow her to leave the house looking like that, regardless of where she may be going, let alone attending church.

"Calm down, dear, the processional is starting; we can talk more about this after church," I said.

At the conclusion of church services each week, Reverend Massy would give announcements and customarily invite everyone to come together for fellowship and enjoin one another for what was supposedly a lite luncheon down in the basement, which was referred to as our "friendship hall." The woman's auxiliary would bring covered casserole dishes that could be placed in the ovens and reheated on low heat to coincide with the end of chapel service. It was anything but a lite luncheon. They prepared everything from simple salads to hearty meat dishes, such as beef stew, goulash, and stroganoff. There was fried chicken, baked fish, and spaghetti— there was only one certainty with confidence each week and that was an over supply of sweets and confections, which, I might add, were always well-received. The average age within the auxiliary was probably close to 70 years. Having that much cooking and baking experience preparing meals for their own families, no one ever knew what concoctions would show up week to week. It actually became an unwritten competition to see who would outshine one another.

After everyone had eaten their fill and talked about everything from local politics to church doctrine, the women would then clear the tables and repackage any food items not eaten. The remaining leftovers were taken down to be shared with the local homeless shelter by our senior men's group, while the young men's forum swept the floor and put away the folding chairs, making sure the friendship hall was neat and orderly for the next activity. Each week,

Abigail and I never planned on preparing a Sunday evening meal, having indulged so excessively earlier in the day.

Sunday was the Lord's Day, a day for reflection, a day of church meetings and chapel services, and a day of renewal by accepting the sacrament of the Eucharist. On Sundays we chose to refrain from any normal day to day activity; no housework, no reviewing of lesson plans, no working in the yard or anything remotely connected to temporal labor; the only exception being was if something was absolutely unavoidable, such as changing a flat tire or climbing up the oak tree in the backyard which Abigail's cat loved to climb, but hadn't as of yet figured out how to get down. Sunday was our day of Sabbath, a day of rest and worship, which we did not take nonchalantly.

Throughout the next week Abigail didn't mention little Allison at all, for which I was extremely grateful, knowing how low-spirited and downhearted she had a tendency to become, especially when something may be contrary to conscience or morality. Having not seen Allison, I wasn't in a position to make comment and I surely wasn't going to tell Abigail what I had found out about her new student after church last Sunday.

Joe Blackwell, our associate pastor, disliked the term, "reverend", believing no man should be revered simply because he is a member of the clergy; and elected not to use that particular word or any nomenclature identifying his work. His primary responsibility was that of our youth chaplain—lovingly nicknamed by our young people in the congregation as "Holy Joe."

During our fellowship luncheon last Sunday Joe took me aside and asked me if I had an apartment rental available. I told him that I sold the apartment building to Jack White some time ago, giving him Jack's telephone number. At that point, Joe went on to say he had a distressing telephone call from Sally Martin, director of the women's shelter "Wings of a Dove", saying she needed help for a young woman and her child. Apparently, the woman had been physically abused by her husband and, although he never hurt the child, the mother feared it was just a matter of time before he did.

"Matthew—the problem is," remarked Joe, "the husband is a police officer who has access to the database of the NCIC, the 'National Crime Information Center' police computer network. Each time she ran away, seeking help from family and friends, he was able to locate her without much difficulty, harassing those who came to her aid even going across state lines."

"That's terrible," I commented.

"Wait, Matthew, there's more. During the past nine years, she had been hospitalized from what Sally told me at least seventeen documented instances, with injuries, ranging from minor contusions, a dislocated shoulder and hip, and twice had her arm was broken, requiring surgical repair. Each time she failed to follow through with criminal charges again her husband out of fear and intimidation," said Joe.

"But why did Sally contact you?" I asked.

"I asked her that," said Joe. "She went on to say that she had heard of my work with young people and felt that maybe I might be able to touch her heart that has become so bitter and cold, untrusting and wary of all persons around her…considering her age. What about her age?"

"Reverend Blackwell," Sally said, "this woman is just barely 20 years old, she became pregnant when she was only 12 by the very same degenerate who has beaten her all these years. She has a daughter by the name of Allison, the cutest little girl you can imagine. Based upon her problems she needs someone who can relate to her age group and possibly instill some measure of trust. She'll trust you above all the social workers and psychologists we have simply because of who you are, a member of the clergy. She says she believes in God, and I'm at the end of my rope trying to find, not only resources, but counseling, as well, to assist her and her child."

"Sally," responded Joe, "I'll make a few phone calls and see what I can do."

"Thank you so much, Reverend Blackwell, I appreciate whatever assistance you can give. This girl just needs some help. One last thing, however, for your information; not only is her husband an alcoholic, he currently is under investigation by federal authorities for civil rights violations of official misconduct of police brutality—facing jail time, himself, vowing to see his wife dead if she testifies against him during his criminal proceedings, reinforcing the attorney general's case of his violence disposition. Knowing what we know, I believe he is indeed capable of carrying out his threats."

"Matthew, please keep this between us," remarked Joe.

"You know you can count on me, Joe," I said, "Did you ever get the woman's name? Didn't you say the daughter's name is Allison?"

"Yes, I did. I believe Sally said her name was Gloria Kory, and your correct the little girl's name is Allison," said Joe.

Knowing my wife as I do—I know she definitely is not an alarmist, and if she felt that something wasn't quite right then there must be something amiss. After speaking with Joe, I have little reason to disbelieve Abigail's sixth sense.

Still I can't help but question in my own heart if maybe, just maybe, she might have some regrets from our discontinuing the in vitro fertilization program attempts and replacing our wanting a child in the hands of God, rather than relying on our unsuccessful continual efforts at Manor General Hospital's infertility clinic. I have asked Abigail repeatedly why she continues teaching a Sunday school class, knowing that personal exposure to the children may have a tendency to bring about unwanted maternalistic feelings, reinforcing the fact that she has never been able to conceive. For the past five or six years she would go in and out of these subjunctive moods of childless desperation, which only time had a way of healing. I did whatever I could to be supportive; I tried validating her role as a good wife, reinforcing her worth, not only as a woman but as a human being. From what I have learned, it is much more difficult for the female counterpart within a marriage to accept not having children than it is on the male. One time she made me promise that whenever she became so fixated on being childless I was to remind her that the main reason she selected to be transferred out of a teaching classroom into school administration was to minimize her exposure to the students she so dearly loved, yet whenever I did as she asked—well, I was the one who suddenly became indifferent.

Her standard response has always been, and I quote, "Matthew— at least I can set an example for my children; it may be the only chance I have to make a real difference in a young person's life."

As each year passed by we reconciled ourselves, speaking less and less about our having a family. We enjoyed the life that God had given us—we have always felt fortunate to have jobs that enabled us to take several mini-vacations yearly, traveling to distant regions of the world; as a general rule of thumb, the week between Christmas and New Year's was used here stateside to visit areas of interest, such as touring the battle sites of the Civil War or visiting the Grand Canyon. We would take an additional ten days or so during the summer months when school was out, which we would extend based upon our itinerary. The year we went to Africa we stayed three weeks.

Each month we posted an average of $1200.00 into a special saving account from our salaries, used exclusively for travel. Any additional monies we might acquire from tutoring or working part-time throughout the year was also earmarked for our excursions.

Whenever asked about our vacation plans there have always been those who thought our method of selection was somewhat odd or indifferent, deviating from what one might expect. To be fair and entirely impartial we came up with a system that eliminates the conflict of I want to go here, you want to go there—now what do we do?

In an old fish bowl we had placed the names of one hundred ninety-two locations throughout the world, based upon the membership of the United Nations; most were individual countries, while some were either territories or under the general provinces of a larger country such as Wales to the United Kingdom. Scotland would be another example. We also included commonwealths, such as Puerto Rico, American Samoa, Guam, the Northern Mariana Islands in Micronesia—halfway between New Guinea and Japan sits the island of Saipan, which we visited one year, and lastly the U.S.

Virgin Islands. In January of each year Abigail would cover her eyes with one hand, place her other hand into the fish bowl and select, at random, one slip of paper—that would be our next port of call for the following year. We would spend hours mulling over each and every brochure or pamphlet we could get our hands on throughout the entire year, contemplating every little detail about our much-anticipated travelogue, which we found to be half the fun. One year, we ended up going on a safari in Zimbabwe, Africa. Another year we went scuba diving off the Great Barrier Reef in Australia. We've backpacked in the green jungle mountains of Costa Rica, cycled our way across Spain picked up a Eurail-Pass and traveled the entire European Continent from north to south and east to west. One summer, we vacationed in Rome, studying religious reference text available to academicians at Vatican City.

In our travel room a world reference map hung on the wall where we had used white plastic push-pins marking each location we had traveled to; a much smaller map of the United States hung over Abigail's desk where she highlighted each state we had visited.

Abigail and I  journeyed to forty-three states, twenty-seven different countries on four separate continents, experiencing life unembellished by tourism. We were so grateful and felt so blessed to have had this opportunity allowing us to feel even closer to God. Thinking back to a verse of scripture, "John 17", where Jesus said, and I'm paraphrasing, "that we should all be as one."

Our friendship and prayer wall in our travel room had hundreds of photographs, mainly of a diverse people worldwide. Wherever we went we kept a daily journal—a written record of experiences and observations, highlighting any information we felt interesting. Without sounding as if we were missionaries, not trying to convert anyone to our beliefs or doctrine, I tried to examine each respective belief within its own social religious culture, and I must admit—I have learned a great deal about religious standards and training from our travels.

On January 27th 1989, my world became isolated between love and hate. Seven months earlier we were informed by" Doctor J" that, after all this time, Abigail and I were to become parents. Abigail was pregnant—we were so ecstatic, almost to the point of disbelief, but it was true…and delighted we were. We were going to have a baby, sadly to say…I eventually deemed her pregnancy a mixed blessing.

Just one week away from our eighteenth anniversary, and one day after the birth of our child my wife, Abigail, died from birth complications. The stress of delivery was simply much more than her frail body could handle, especially having survived the massive cancer treatments. Having a baby in your mid-forties can be difficult, to say the least, but especially so if it is your first delivery and your general heath is weakened.

There must have been a very special reason for placing this child in our care; after all, God could have placed her with another family with a much younger set of parents. Whatever his foresight, my wife and I were grateful for her special, charitable spirit.

# Chapter 2: A Life of Love

I knew that life was not going to be easy raising a child as a single father. Abigail and I never had other children, so it was trial and error all along the way. We had been married since our graduate years from Maryland Christian University and had planned for our future as well as anyone could have. We made arrangements for everything well in advance; retirement, insurance and, in general, our well-being for our golden years. We thought we had made provisions for everything, everything that is, except the trials that had been placed before us during Abigail's illness. Even before we married we spoke about the joys and comfort of having a family, a son—a daughter or perhaps even twins, since identical twins ran in both sides of our families. For the last twelve years or so neither one of us had even contemplated the idea of raising children. We simply accepted the fact that, for whatever the reasons, Abigail never became pregnant. At that point of time we never questioned the reason why we didn't have children; we both believed that if it were meant to be, it would happen.

Long before Abigail was diagnosed as having osteogenic sarcoma we discussed the role that death plays within human life. We accepted the placement of death in man's life as part of God's finite plan. We accepted death on face value based upon our faith with a knowing that we would eventually be together—reunited for all time and eternity whenever our time came.

Four months after Abigail was diagnosed as having cancer, we were blessed with the news that we were going to be parents. The doctors assured us that since Abigail had completed her final stage of radiation therapy they saw no reason for concern where the pregnancy was concerned.

We were so delighted with the pregnancy—to think, after all this time we were finally going to have a child, a responsibility that neither one of us would take lightly. Abigail and I daydreamed about what it was going to be like raising a son or daughter, taking care to always refer to our unborn child in a neutral-sex setting. It didn't matter to either one of us whether we had a boy or a girl; as long as he or she was healthy and had two arms, two legs, eight fingers and two thumbs, and so on.

Throughout the pregnancy Abigail was compelled to have an ultrasound examination on a regular basis—every five or six weeks as a safety precaution, to measure the blood flow through our baby's heart. Dr. McKnight—Abigail's obstetrician, explained that it was a safeguard to view any abnormality that might develop from Abigail's previous chemotherapy.

Although we had chosen not to ask the sex of our unborn child, an overzealous ultrasound technician, not knowing our wishes, blurted out in Abigail's third month, "Oh my…what a perfect little girl." Abigail and I looked at each other and laughed, agreeing that it was a matter of karma.

Raising a child with Abigail would have been a great joy that she and I would have shared together. To do so without her simply never entered my mind. Nevertheless, I was not ready for this.

I gave my soul completely in my early teen years to an assemblage of different religious values. My mother was brought up within Jewish Orthodoxy and my father's family was hard-core Southern Baptist. Based solely upon my mother's lineage by birthright I, too, am Jewish. At the age of six, my parents enrolled me in a Catholic parochial school system where I remained under the strict guidance of Jesuit teachings through my graduation year at age sixteen. They did so merely because of their each devout theism and couldn't agree as to my religious upbringing. Furthermore, to complicate my religious upbringing even more so, as a preschool youngster we lived in a predominately Asian community where the majority of my friends were either *Nisei* or *Sansei* second or third generation Japanese Americans—so for the most part, my friends and playmates were Zen Buddhist who practiced enlightenment through meditation, emphasizing physical and spiritual discipline as a means of interpreting the world around them, rather than a faith in a supreme being.

I can't say I wasn't confused—because for the longest of time I considered myself to be an outsider from any mainstream religious movement. Eventually, I realized that there was some truth in all beliefs with regard to a supreme deity. I chose to view life not only from a Christian point of view but followed some of the teachings of the Buddha and the sacred writing of the Talmud. As I grew older, my inquisitiveness led me to studies from various sacred texts of eastern sects, including that of Hinduism and Islam teachings from the Quran.

Knowing that so much truth has been rewritten, transliterated from language to language and hidden from mankind in general by so-called organized religion, I began early on to believe that we each must learn what we can, accepting what we believe to be good and discounting the negative. There were so many gospels written that gave truth, which we as humankind will never be able to read because some church leaders in the first and second century deemed it confusing or perhaps adjudged the writings to be without merit. It's sad to think that some of God's eternal truths were lost due to man's inability to sanctify writings from what was considered conventional orthodox heresy. It has only been through my independent study and examination of various churches conjoined with resolute prayer that has allowed me to become the man that I am today.

I'm anything but Job, an Old Testament Jewish leader who maintained his faith in God in spite of the afflictions that God sent his way. I'm simply a man who believes in God, trying my best not to practice sin and to live my life by the example of my savior Jesus Christ. Yet, even with my belief system, I have never been able to answer why such a loving God would allow such unpleasant things to happen? To take my life-long companion, my only true love. To take the only woman I have ever known and replace her with an infant, especially at my age, to nurture all alone. Why…I questioned times untold.

I knew little about raising a child, especially a baby girl. I had never changed a diaper, didn't even know how to properly hold her, let alone how to prepare baby formula or provide for her needs. Sleep had become my nemesis, and when I was able to drift off I would only catnap to awaken abruptly, dreaming of the countless mistakes I might potentially make. Countless times each day I wondered how I could go on without my dear Abigail.

I prayed and cried, and cried and prayed. Finally, it was not until I surrendered and relinquished my pride and anger against God that allowed me a level of acceptance to find comfort and spiritual support and accept the custodianship of my daughter.

Dr. Shaw a pediatric resident told me that my child would have to remain in the hospital nursery for approximately ten days. He assured me that she was fine, just a bit under-weight. The nursing staff explained that she would be well taken care of, allowing me the time frame to make the necessary arrangements to take her home after Abigail's memorial. Having to deal with two major life crises coincidentally was, without question, overwhelming.

The night of Abigail's interment was the hardest night I could have ever imagined. The house had been full of friends and colleagues the entire day. After everyone had gone, I walked through each room of the house, trying to pickup and straighten whatever disarray I found. Finally it hit me, a total feeling of emptiness inside—unlike anything I had every known. The reality had set in; I was all alone and Abigail was gone. I was frightened, knowing full well that I must now face the world without my beloved wife. I felt as if my life was over and yet something deep down inside of me kept saying that it was just beginning. I realized that Abigail's likeness lived on in our precious daughter; even at birth, she resembled her mother completely. I also knew that this child, this tiny baby girl desperately needed me. Still, I questioned if I could be strong enough to raise a child by myself.

As I entered the baby's room I picked up a small satin pillow that Abigail had placed in a rocking chair next to the crib. Abigail worked endlessly preparing the nursery. She had it painted a pretty pale pink with a cherub theme; angels were everywhere, from the contrasting wallpaper boarder to the illuminating nightlight. In one of the many baby stores she frequented, she found a reprint of Monet's Guardian Angel, which she purchased and hung on the wall just above the creamed-colored canopy crib of lace. She made certain everything was just right for the baby we would soon be bringing home. We were both so overjoyed about the gift that we would soon be receiving, the gift of life from our Father in Heaven.

I remember my mother saying that, "Men make plans and God only laughs." For me, personally, I chose to think that this time he only cried.

I found myself sitting in the middle of the floor, clutching that small satin pillow that Abigail had made, sobbing for the loss of my wife. What's remarkable, I remember thinking, is that Abigail didn't sew. She couldn't replace a button if it was missing from one of my shirts, let alone cutout and sew from a pattern a baby's first pillow. I laughed and teased her when she first started that project, as only a husband could do. Abigail was the perfect wife and a great housekeeper, but by no means handy with a needle and thread. To my surprise she did a remarkable job making that pillow; she wanted to give something special to her baby, something handmade that perhaps she would, in turn, hand-down to her child someday. As I held onto that pillow I cried so hard that I had fallen asleep from sorrow and grief, but by the grace of God had awakened with a newness of purpose.

I have never mentioned this to a living soul, but Abigail came to me that night in a dream. She was dressed in radiant white with a luminescence and warmth about her. Abigail told me that I had to let her memory go and accept the responsibility that God himself gave me. She told me that he never would have entrusted our baby in my care if he didn't think that I could handle the job. She continued on by saying that her love would always be ever-present and that the spirit of life would indeed be there to help me along the way. Abigail assured me that our religious beliefs and values were just and true, that the love of God was never-ending. She also said that the day would come that we would once again be reunited as a complete family within the body of Christ, quoting a verse in the Old Testament from the book of Jeremiah. I know it sounds strange, but when I awoke I wasn't the slightest bit apprehensive or afraid. I had total recall of Abigail's spirit and the meaning she left behind. My mind, body, and spirit felt renewed, I knew what I needed to do; I prayed and asked for guidance with a newness of heart and went straightway to the hospital to see my precious baby daughter.

Upon entering the hospital, I proceeded to the nurse's station in the neonatal care unit and asked the charge nurse to see my daughter, requesting that the name-tag around her tiny wrist, which read, "Baby Anderson", be replaced with a chosen first name of "Abby", after her mother.

Mrs. Simmons, the charge nurse on duty, directed me to the hospital nursery where she sat me down in the rocking chair, placing a pale pink baby blanket on my lap adjacent to an empty bassinet; she directed one of the nursing aides to bring my baby to me. The aide handed Abby to Mrs. Simmons who, in turn, positioned her just so in my lap, instructing me to place my bent arm beneath the back of her neck giving support. I sat there mesmerized holding Abby for the very first time with great fear and in a cold sweat. She was so small and fragile and yet determined to survive despite her delicate size. I knew I held a part of my wife as I sat there holding my daughter, asking God in silent prayer for his help in raising this child.

It has been nine years now since Abigail has been gone. I know I have made my share of mistakes raising Abby; it's not been easy and, at times, even unpleasant, but for the most part quite enjoyable. She and I have become much more than father and daughter, we have become the best of friends. In many ways, she is much older than her tender years suggest and she, too, has become over-protective of me as I have always been of her.

I have raised Abby with more than just a set of moral values of rights and wrongs; I have attempted to inspire, by personal example, a sense of humanistic understanding for all humankind, male or female, ingraining equality in all things.

With one exception, I have never deliberately lied to Abby. Her mother, my dearest Abigail died without warning from a weak heart; cardiomyopathy is what the doctor's said. The stress from childbirth just caused her heart to give out. The only time I have ever told Abby a half-truth was when she asked about her mother's death. I told her that her mother died when she was just a baby, from a simple heart attack. She understood that. I couldn't bear to be truthful, but chose to lie by omission, using deception for what I believed to be the right reasons, knowing full well that her mother died as a result of her pregnancy.

From the time she was first able to talk, she and I developed an understanding that truth would always be foremost in our relationship. She's never told me a falsehood—right, wrong or indifferent, she never made excuses for her actions. As a parent, being truthful to a child is not always easy.

Abby and I have never missed church attendance and I'm certain it is one of the reasons her value system is as strong as it is. She is as knowledgeable about the Bible as any adolescent could be, she may not fully understand its conceptual meaning or precepts just yet, but does indeed know of its guiding principles.

I've never been afraid to talk with Abby about anything; sometimes I wonder if she hadn't missed her childhood altogether being the progeny of a single father. First it was pre-k, then first grade, second grade and then, before I knew it, she was acting as if she were about to graduate from high school. I never intended it to be that way—she just assimilated into being such a young adult, rather than allowing herself to act as a child.

Abby has always had a way of discernment—a way of understanding, now—to ask her to react to this dreaded disease as an adult, to ask her to lessen the intensity, the anxieties and fears of having leukemia is greater than I can bear at times. Her mother would surely be proud of the way she has held up, I know I certainly am.

I recognized a long time ago that God only allows us to care for his children as mortal parents. We don't own them, they're not ours, and we're just his custodians until the time comes that they must return to him in Paradise. Every parent hopes that their own time will come before their child's does. Life is His to give or take, according to His wishes and needs. We know this, but it doesn't make it any easier to find acceptance during times of calamity.

It is extremely difficult, living in this temporal body, to accept the divine will of God. I pray for the courage and strength to face what I now must encounter; Abby has become ill and her state of health is also in his hands. She is barely holding on to each day—grasping to an unknown time frame. As I held her hand, day after day sitting by her bedside, I wondered how much longer I could remain strong for her benefit. It's anything but easy being the parent of a dying child, searching to find reason and acceptance. Losing my life's partner was dreadful, but now to lose my child is unimaginable. Abby floats in and out of a stupor, somewhat in a daze. The doctors and nurses have made her as comfortable as humanly possible; time has not only become our enemy, but our advocate as well. Her leukemia has advanced to its final stages where the only thing keeping her alive is the Devine will of God.

As a parent, I hope and pray for remission; thinking somehow, somewhere, a new medical breakthrough will be developed. Deep in my heart I know full-well the odds of finding such a cure in her lifetime are hopeless, but I still hope, nonetheless. God must have his reasons and it's not my place to question his will.

Being the only child of a single parent, Abby gave me great joy and happiness. I have learned that child rearing is no easy task and respect motherhood as never before, having walked in her shoes. If it were not for my caring friends and neighbors, I don't know how I could have survived the many pitfalls of single fatherhood. Children go in and out of various stages of life, trying to fit-in, reaching a stabilized level of their own independence. One moment Abby would crawl upon my lap just needing to be held, the next moment she was much to grown up for that sort of thing. She had always been an active little girl, full of playfulness and love, the compassion within her heart, especially where animals were concerned, would put Saint Francis of Assisi to shame.

Abby's schedule kept me busy, much more than I would have liked. Monday night each week was her tumbling class, the next night was her ballet practice—not to forget any recital that came along from time to time. The Girl Scouts added yet another evening of required participation, followed generally by some sort of activity on the weekends. Every Sunday afternoon following church services Abby and the other young girls in the auxiliary league volunteered to hand-out newspapers and magazines at the nursing home.

I'm ashamed to say, but there were times that I hated her popularity and her wanting to participate in everything. If ever a little girl loved life, certainly it was my Abby.

Thinking back now, I feel guilty having not allowed some of the activities she treasured so. How I wish I could once again drive her and her friends to a birthday party, or perhaps to the movies or ice skating.

There were times that it was nothing less than my fears that kept some activities at bay, like the time her Girl Scout troop went rock climbing and I made up the excuse that we were going out of town to visit her grandmother, and that her "Granny M" would be so disappointed if we were to cancel the plans we already made. The truth was—I was afraid, afraid she might fall, prompting a little white lie. One little white lie always led to another—it then became necessary to telephone Abigail's mother just in case Abby were to speak to her, which in turn may have placed her in the position of supporting my falsehood.

Watching Abby draw nearer to death each day took its toll. I, too, lived in a stupor. In contrast, however, I was able to walk about in good health. I pled with God to allow Abby to live—regain her health, and take my life instead. During each day she was only awake a few hours, how I learned to cherish what little time we had. I know that with her medication her pain was minimal; however, any pain to a child can be devastating for any parent. As her father I couldn't help it. I had an innate tendency to safeguard, to nurture and protect. This feeling of hopelessness was overwhelming. Now that Abby was over the final suffering stages, I too was the one who was suffering,

suffering because of my helplessness. There was not a single thing that I could do to help my daughter; each day, watching her slip further away from me became increasingly intense. What little time we shared daily gave comfort to my broken heart, despite the intense anger I was feeling.

Once again, I kept trying to find some rational reason why this had happened to my daughter. I knew I hadn't the right to question the divine will of God, but after all I was only human. I realized I was not the first parent to go through this, but still questioned repeatedly—why me?

My belief is God is beyond reproach; I tithe above the customary percentage and truly care about my fellow man. I always considered Abby to be a very special gift, a gift from God. Once again I question why would God honor me with such a precious gift, only then…to play take away?

Having a great deal of time on my hands sitting by Abby's bedside, I became aware and mindful of the facts—how the *why me* developed and became a fixation. Not only did I question the reasons why, I also began to have doubts about what I truly believed in. *Tragedies like this happen to other families, other people, but not to me! I am a good Christian, then again—why me, why my daughter? Why? Why? Why?*

The more I thought about my discomfort the more I realized that I had found a level of acceptance with Abby's illness. God has a way of permitting each of us to find, even in the most devastating of situations, a haven of accepting the unacceptable. I finally understood that questioning the divine will of God is only natural. At first I thought it to be a sin, now I know better. Sitting here day after day allows a great deal of time to ponder the great mysteries of life, you can't help but think, that's all you can do, everything else in life seems to be a distraction. You're afraid to leave their room because your child might awaken, even if only to grab a quick bite to eat or go to the restroom. Everything, and I mean everything, in life now takes a back seat to spending time with your child. The bills mount up, but you justify to yourself that someday you will get caught up.

Finally, you get to a point where you place blame upon yourself. You think…God is certainly punishing me for something I must have done. But what could I have done to demerit such stigma?

Then, when you ultimately reach a point where nothing else makes any sense, you blame God.

Soon afterwards I found myself trying to bargain with God, thinking God is sympathetic and compassionate, he knows what would be in my best interest—certainly not that of taking my child. God knows my heart and mind, my wants, needs and desires. The mere fact in knowing that there is opposition in all things didn't help either. I found little solace knowing that Satan has a way of promoting and prompting ideas in our minds. Once we each recognize our *mind talk* is always 99.9% a lie, we can go on, ask for forgiveness and strive yet another day.

I never realized how time could drag on so. It was the longest twenty-nine months in my life, yet, in so many ways, the shortest. I will always carry a bit of grief, emptiness within my soul, which can only be replenished from the memories of my precious daughter. Yet, within that void, I will also carry joy; a joy in the knowing that my child has been reunited with her mother and the Blessed Trinity.

Christ himself taught that there are many great mysteries that will not be understood until his return. King Solomon wrote in the Old Testament of the Christian Bible—that upon our deaths our spirits return to God. The prophet Muhammad stated in the Quran—the primary text of Islam—that Muslims believe that death is a departure from the life of this world, but not the end of a person's existence. The Torah actually states that death is a good thing, and the doctrine of an afterlife in heaven with God Almighty is a fundamental Jewish belief. Personally, I know I haven't all the answers and choose to believe that when we die—we are reunited with our heavenly families who have gone before us to a place called paradise, where our souls experience unimaginable pleasures, for all time and eternity, having a direct closeness to God.

Confronting the imminent death of a family member, especially that of a child, is overwhelming. Not only must we accept the loss of a loved one, but must do so holding on to apprehensions from the unknown. All religious tenets, regardless of the doctrine are based upon faith; yet, the humanistic side of being mortal dedicates that no one has ever been there and returned with a complete description of what dead is.

Remember the last Thanksgiving holiday Abby and I shared together, I spent the better part of a day with the help of a nurse or two, decorating Abby's hospital room with the customary festive array of posters, streamers, and foldout paper figurines. I wanted her to know that when she awoke, I was there to share our holiday blessings, as we always had. I will never forget the look on her face when she opened her little eyes and saw a life-sized, blown-up vinyl turkey sitting on her bedside table. She smiled with such warm-heartedness and actually held a glow about her face. Abby knew I was there—that's all she needed, she closed her eyes not to awaken until the following day.

"Dad," she said, "I had the craziest dream last night. You and I were sitting around our dining room table at home; the table was full of our favorite foods; mashed potatoes, candied yams, cornbread stuffing, cranberry sauce, pumpkin pie and a pitcher of lemonade. Next to the pitcher of lemonade were three empty glasses filled with ice, the only thing I didn't see was the turkey. It wasn't in the center of the table where we always place it—then all of a sudden, some real pretty lady with long blond hair walked in from the kitchen carrying a platter with the biggest turkey I had ever seen. She sat it down in from of you, gave you a kiss on the cheek and asked you to give the blessing. She walked back into the kitchen and was gone and never returned. I didn't get a look at her face; oh yeah, I also heard church music playing from the kitchen. What a weird dream—we never ate a bite, but we were together. It was really kinda nice. I just can't figure-out who that pretty lady was."

Days drifted one into another, each day as the day before, thwarting off death with great vengeance. It was a waiting game and with each passing days my hopes diminished. I knew my child was not going to get better. Knowing it was just a matter of time, still I did not want to accept the inevitable. The nursing staff did everything in their power to give me as much latitude as possible. They were each so kind and caring, developing a unique kinship with Abby as if she were the only patient they had. One thing was certain; Abby received the very best of medical care, quite simply because it was truly given under the auspices of love.

For Christmas I hired a shopping service to buy gifts for Abby. I just could not bring myself to leave her bedside. I knew that she would never use or play with the gifts and toys they purchased, but still, I had to give her a Christmas even in the hospital. I decided that afterwards I would donate whatever the service acquired to the children's ward. I had to make a number of concessions and adjustments in my lifestyle. For starters, I took a leave of absence from my job and then refinanced our home. The first thing that any parent of a terminally ill child needs to do is to minimize the worry about financial matters. I sat with the doctor's and asked questions pertaining to Abby's illness. They were hard but necessary, nonetheless, pertaining to timelines, keeping in mind a great many questions were, in fact, conjecture. I needed to know where I stood and what I was dealing with. In many ways it seemed rather cold and callous; still, medical care, like everything else in life, has a business side. Expenditures must be met, a fiscal plan, not only for the medical expenses not covered by insurance, but for my incidental living expenses, as well. I had to keep in mind that life goes on even in the face of death. Taxes become due, mortgages must be met, insurance payments and everyday living expenses have to be accounted for.

I stood at the window in Abby's room and looked out at a hazy blue-gray sky, thinking that winter was a bit late this year. I watched a single snowflake fall and became mesmerized with its movement. Each year Abby would become so excited when she noticed the first signs of approaching ski season. If ever a child loved the snow, it was my daughter, Abby.

So much had happened, so much had changed. Two years ago at this time I never would have thought that I would be standing here in this hospital room praying for my daughter's life. Life can change ever so quickly without our realizing it. Last Winter I recall how thrilled and electrified Abby became when she told me that she had learned that no two snowflakes were exactly the same. Abby had always had an inquisitive mind, with a remarkable quest for knowledge. As amazing as it may sound, she even questioned her approaching death with the same vigor, not what you might expect, especially from a child barely twelve years old. In a philosophical way, she queried the nature of life, the purpose of existence and her own mortality in a secular sort of way. She never questioned God's judgment or his intent, but questioned the why…behind the pain and suffering for humankind, in general. Abby knew she was dying, and only once can I recall her ever using the word dying with reference to herself. I have refrained from using such words as *death* or *dying* because they have such a negative connotation. Abby's death would be anything but negative.

The New Year had come and gone and yet Abby still held on. The doctor's and staff could give no sound logical explanation as to why she was still alive; she had out-lived the timeframe given by three different oncology specialists. I had no doubt in my heart that she was only alive but by the grace of God. Her disease had indirectly affected every major organ of her ailing body; her general condition was just barely above that of necessitating the use a life support system. Her breathing was shallow and erratic; her temperature would spike—rarely falling below 102 degrees.

Cheryl Anne, a much caring hospice charge nurse who worked the midnight shift, came to me after a rather rough night, asking if I had ever considered euthanasia. I knew she meant well, and genuinely cared for Abby, sad, but she had no idea of what she suggested. Later that morning after LaDonna arrived, I found out that Cheryl had lost a child, too, some years previous and had dedicated herself to children with terminal diseases. It is obvious by her mere question that she had no religion or belief system separating life and death. To her, they were one in the same. Cheryl could only see the pain and suffering of her patients and admittedly believed that God did not exist.

Since she held no belief system in a living God nor understood why any sensible person could have, she was reluctant to open discussions concerning religious creeds and doctrine. I tried to explain the nature and makeup of God and the Holy Trinity; at various times I felt that she wasn't being receptive to the meanings of my message. However, despite the fact that I was tired, much too tired and consumed with Abby's needs to even think about saintly teachings, I do believe I did my best under the circumstances.

I informed Cheryl that God has to need no calculate any measurement of time, at least, not in the way that we do, explaining that God has always been, and always will be. I gave quotes paraphrasing the Old Testament where God referred to Himself as the great "I Am", hoping that she could conceive of God as being omnipresent, illuminating the fact that He never referred to Himself as the "I Was", or "I Will Be", but an entity of existence in the present and now. I tried to explain that believing in a supreme being is quite different and unique for each of us, and must be done so voluntarily, explaining the concept of "freewill." To accept Jesus as the Christ is a very personal matter and can only be accomplished out of faith—without tangible evidence. I explained that for me it was just an innate knowing that Christ is, always has been and always will be, period. My needing proof has never been part of the equation.

Using Abby's illness symbolically I said, "Cheryl, if it were not for my daughter's illness, we would not be sitting here now having this discussion." I also explained that it is written in the scriptures that when two or more are gathered in his name, he will be there also. "So you see Cheryl, God is here—right now," I said, "we can't see his presence in a physical realm, but we have a knowing that his presence is here. It's what we call faith; being able to believe in something we can't possibly explain. Having faith is the substance of just knowing, without having proof. God loves each and every one of us the same, he always has and he always will. Personally, I don't need to have any proof that he exists, I just know that he does. Cheryl, look at it this way, maybe—just maybe, God is utilizing Abby's condition as a means of providing you a time to search your heart and mind, hoping that you will return to him with a renewed faith. Remember what I said, we never would have met if my daughter had never become ill."

"Look, Matthew," Cheryl said, "I haven't the time for this; quite frankly I consider it a waste of your time trying to convince me otherwise. Look, I understand what you are saying, and it's okay for you to believe as you do. But for me, I just can't comprehend it. If he were real, how he could allow terrible things to happen, especially to children. I just can't accept it! The belief in this so-called 'God-Being' was conceived by the imagination of men to be able to accept the unacceptable, that's all there is to it! Facts are facts, one moment we're born—the next moment we die. Believe me—all we have is what we make it in-between. Your God allowed my daughter, Tina, to die, just as he is allowing your daughter, Abby, to do. Do you honestly think that God is going to perform a miracle and save your daughter? I don't think so! You can't possibly understand how I feel, Matthew, you really can't."

"Cheryl, I know what you're saying," I said, "but I also know, by your own admission, that you really do believe in God."

"I didn't say that! Where did that come from? On the contrary I know he doesn't exist—He just couldn't! Matthew, like I said, your God is nothing more than wishful thinking in your own imagination. Can't you really see that by your believing in some sort of a supreme being, that by itself, allows you a venue to accept the unacceptable," she replied.

"Cheryl, deep in your heart you know without a doubt, that God is real. In your own words, you said that 'He' allowed Tina to die, you also said that 'He' could have saved her, but didn't. Can't you see by your own admission that you do acknowledged the existence of God, if by no other means instinctively then. Words are very powerful, in the Bible it talks about the power of the tongue. Someday, if you would like, we can talk about it. Believing in God is just a knowing whether you what to admit it to yourself or not. Cheryl, if you're so adamant about your non-belief in God, please explain to me how you could blame him for your daughter's death," I asked.

Without saying a word, Cheryl abruptly got up from her seat and ran out of the room as she began to cry. She didn't need to say anything; it wasn't hard to see that the hand of God had touched her soul. I didn't see Cheryl for the next few days and wondered if my zeal hadn't aroused her anger instead of promoting a line of thought. When we did meet up with one another, before I had a chance to speak to her, she blurted out almost uncontrollably, thanking me for the time we spent together—adding that she spent a lot of time thinking since we first met and finally realized how clueless she was with respect to God's plan. She went on to ask if it were appropriate to pray to angels, especially her guardian angel.

Her new demeanor was certainly refreshing and enthusiastic, making way for still other questions in her life.

"Matthew, what do I do next? I know now there is a God and that he loves me, but how can I learn more about God and his teachings? How can I find out what his plan is for me?" she asked.

"Now slowdown, Cheryl," I said, "I know that you're excited and I can't blame you, but Rome wasn't built in a day and neither will be your learning of Godly things. From here on, it's baby-steps…you must first learn to crawl before you learn to walk, let alone learn to run. Rest assured, God, with His infinite wisdom and perfect timing, knows your heart and mind and will create a learning path that's just right for you. Stay close in prayer, talk to him as if you were talking to me.

We made plans to get together the following week. After Cheryl left, I took a reclusive moment for myself cloistered in the linen closet down the hallway to give thanks for that Spirit within me, having been given the appropriate choice of words that she so desperately needed to hear. At that same moment my mind wandered off, thinking how very fragile our belief system can be; *That is even one more reason*, I thought to myself, *to give thanks to my Heavenly Father for giving me a sound mind not closed to sacred mysteries or understandings*—thinking back to the Bible verse in Jeremiah 31:33.

Later that same day I walked into a conversation at the nursing station—not meaning to eavesdrop—but overheard several of the nurses and aides making plans to have a little birthday celebration for one of their own, as it turned out…it was for Cheryl.

That next Thursday around noontime, Cheryl and I met as agreed and had a quick lunch while Abby was bathing and having her massage. When Cheryl arrived at Abby's room, before going downstairs to the cafeteria, I reached down in my overnight bag and retrieved a small parcel wrapped in plain Manila paper tied with cotton twine.

As we ate our lunch, I purposely refrained from talking about religion or the powers that control human destiny, steering our conversation to a more personal setting; wanting to know more about her personal life, religious values and what religious instruction she may have had, thinking the present I was about to give her might well be a good starting point for her discovery.

"Cheryl," I said, "I have a little birthday present for you, one I hope you will use."

"Matthew," she responded, "how did you know it was my birthday? Actually, it was yesterday, forty-nine years old," she chuckled.

I handed her the present I had wrapped, it wasn't very neat—gift wrapping has always been somewhat difficult for me, the paper never seems to line-up as it should and the ends, well, they tend to look as if a primate had wrapped them. As she began to open the small unadorned package I had given her, tears started rolling down her cheeks. Without saying a word, she read the card I had hand written and placed within the package.

> *Cheryl, just a little something to say thank you for all you have done for my daughter. I am so very grateful for your delightful spirit. As you can see, the outside overall wrapping is rather quite simple and plain, no frills, bows or ribbons. This was done so to stress the fact that external judgments be they simplistic or elaborate can be deceiving. Upon opening its contents you will find three distinct books, each wrapped in different colored paper,*

*establishing that they are indeed separate, yet collectively universal one to another. When you read and study, read not only with your eyes, but listen to what you have read with your heart. May these books, along with your prayers, guide you in your quest for knowledge. Have a happy birthday, my friend.*

As she opened the package, she gently folded the wrapping paper of each text, placing it within the back cover jacket. The first book she opened was a copy of the Kings James Version of the Holy Bible; the second book was a book of Jewish commentaries on the Torah, and the third book, a book of sacred text from the Quran.

"Matthew," she said, "I don't know what to say…I mean, just to say thank you—doesn't seem to be enough, I have never had anyone give me anything with so much thought attached. Would you mind, if, I still came to you for advice? I mean, I really don't know how to use these books; is there one I should read before the other?"

"Cheryl, the books that I've given you are a lifetime study; keep in mind from the beginning of time, there have been countless volumes written about man and his search for religious truth. The only true question I see is…its authenticity.

"I've read various opinions advocating that the Bible isn't trustworthy enough believing, that some books were removed from it; then again there are those who would fight to the death in opposition. Frankly, I just don't know about the claims that some people have made; debating that the Bible was edited by early church leaders, who removed information they felt inappropriate for whatever their reasoning. If, by chance, an ancient writing showed some sort of abstract contention, giving argument with historical inaccuracies, or perhaps somehow gave contrary opinion to church doctrine, then I could see how it might be omitted. Like I said, I just don't know; what I do know, however, is that I believe that we will each be judged based upon what information we have. Cheryl, keep in mind as you begin your research and study, whatever you may read from whatever the source, 'gospel truism' cannot contradict itself, it is either true or false and cannot be both at the same time.

"There are many ancient writings written around the same timeframe when the Bible was written. For me, I personally choose to neither accept nor reject anything they impart. Just recently with all of the hullabaloo about Jesus having a wife, come on, would it really make a difference if he were married one way or another, I think not. Do you understand what I am saying? Read what you will; find something in the index of the Bible that arouses your interest then cross-reference the same subject matter in perhaps the Torah or Quran. As you progress in obtaining biblical information, or rather, I should say, obtaining authenticated records documented by fact, you'll find yet additional sources of text that will just blow you away. The fact is…you must find out for yourself what is truth for you."

"But Matthew," Cheryl said, "I'm already lost and I haven't even begun. Won't you please help me? Oh my God, look at the time, we've got to go. Abby is going to wonder what has taken us so long."

As I stood up from my chair, gathering my thoughts, I said, "Cheryl, are you ready for lesson one? Never, and I do mean never, use the name of the Lord our God in any circumstance other than in worship speaking directly to him. I told you before how powerful words are, and to call upon the Lord by using his name apart from giving praise, well, it should never be done. In Judaism, for example, the name of God is more than an identifying factor, his name represents the concept of divine nature—giving and showing a respect and reverence for his holiness. The various names we use in representation of the supreme being of God be they—Lord Almighty, Jehovah or Yahweh must always demonstrate divine respect."

# Chapter 3: A Dilemma of Choice

My leave of absence from work was about up and either I must return to my job or simply resign my teaching position. The school district that I had worked for the past twenty-one years had been more than supportive; it had been over a year, either leave Abby's bedside or forfeit my post. The only other option I had was to apply for early retirement. Whatever I decided, it had to be one that would afford me the luxury of maintaining my insurance policy, regardless.

I have been a teacher my entire life, it has always been the only occupation that I had ever contemplated. Abigail and I met while attending teacher's college at the University of Maryland. Helping young minds to grow and expand was a lifelong dream that we shared together. I thank God every day for having nurtured my interest as a child to the humanities; being a teacher has ultimately given me the independent freedom to raise Abby by myself without the aid of a live-in housekeeper. Once Abby had started school, she and I were away for virtually the same hours each day.

Having to be both roles of a mother and a father to a young child is time consuming at best, with needs that must be met from the early morning hours each day, preparing breakfast to the evening ritual of bathing, homework, and nightly prayer. I simply can't fathom the idea of any parent trying to raise a child having irregular work hours. I decided that I would do whatever was necessary, no matter the cost. Sometimes in life we have to make unpleasant decisions that are morally correct. I hated the idea of having to leave teaching at this time. My students had suffered enough having substitute replacements during my absence; most substitute teachers, through no fault of their own, are lacking—not that they don't care, they simply haven't the time to become part of each class they monitor. Each and every one of my students knows me; they know what I expected and what we must accomplish before the end of each term, with no excuses for mismanagement of time or frolic in my classroom. I maintained a personalized contract with all of my students, allowing a *quid pro quo* from term to term. Substitute teachers haven't the time allowance to see the transformation from a mental slate once void of equation to the overflowing of data of a young mind finally reaching that level of knowing.

I can't say I haven't missed my class; on the contrary, I have truly missed each one of my students along with their personalities—behaviorally, temperamentally and emotionally. My kids were unique individuals. Just knowing I had a hand in their growth and development was blessing enough for me. However, right now I had to concentrate on Abby and her needs.

It's difficult to comprehend how rapidly cancer can grow in the human body; it's even harder to believe how little we know with understanding about this dreadful disease. We have the knowledge and capability to send men to outer space, to build underground cities and tunnels under the oceans. We have the ability to duplicate matter, to decipher and unravel complex structures as the DNA of human life. Yet, we haven't a clue as to the cause and cures of various cancers.

When Abby first became ill, I thought it only to be a slight cold, possibly influenza. She had the usual symptoms of fever, body aches and overall fatigue. I knew she was really ill when she had lost her appetite—Abby loved to eat. Unlike me she could eat anything; I look at food and gain weight, she, on the other hand, could eat double portions and never gain an ounce, Abigail was like that, too.

On the third day of her general discomfort—seeing that, if anything, she was getting worst—I called Dr. Jenkins and made an appointment for the next morning, I also telephoned Mrs. Koenig, the school secretary, asking her to find a substitute for my classes for the remainder of the week. I explained that Abby had picked-up some sort of virus and I wouldn't be in. I knew it wasn't any of the common health problems that children get; she'd had the mumps, measles, and chicken pox. She wasn't having any intestinal problems and, in general, Abby was quite healthy.

Later that same night, just past midnight, Abby spiked a fever of 102 degrees. Immediately, I called Dr. Jenkins' night service and, within minutes, Dr. Jenkins' returned my telephone call, saying he would be right over. Mark Jenkins, referred to as simply *Dr. J*, was a close friend of many years; actually he was Abigail's family physician when she was a child. I know he had to be well into his 70s, but was as fit and agile as a young man of 30. He played golf and tennis twice a week, whenever his time permitted. He was an old-fashioned family practitioner, a doctor that even made house calls in this day and age. He said that it didn't sound serious, give her plenty of liquids and bed rest and a large dish of ice cream when the patient felt up to it. He advised me that he would stop over on his way home tomorrow evening, assuring me that he had recently seen a dozen other children with the same symptoms.

I remembered Abby lifting her head off the pillow and smiling in both our directions. I thanked him for coming by and asked if I needed to get a prescription filled or anything. Mark shook his head no and said that the only thing she needed was simply some rest, that time was the best healing medicine available.

The next morning Abby wasn't any better. She was soaking wet from perspiration, having bouts of hot and cold chills. I called Mark at his office and he advised me that, although he didn't think it any great concern, but to go ahead and bring her in and he would look at her once again. This time when he saw Abby, I could see concern on his face contemplating it to be more than a mere childhood illness. Mark commented that he wanted to run some blood work and when the results came back from the lab, we would know more. After the exam I took Abby home and awaited Dr. Jenkins's call.

About 2:30 P.M. that Thursday afternoon, Mark's nurse telephoned indicating that she had already made arrangements to admit Abby to the regional medical center. She said that Dr. Jenkins would meet us there, to go straightway to the emergency room where he would be awaiting to admit her directly from there.

I knew my asking the customary whys and wherefores would be of no avail. Doctors and nurses, in general, are notorious for saying very little having a tendency to be extremely tightlipped.

Within thirty minutes we were at the hospital; within forty-five minutes Abby was admitted and in her room. Little did I know that she would be compelled to remain in that room for the next eleven months.

Before Dr. Jenkins had arrived, a laboratory technician came in and drew even more blood samples from Abby, she was so sick; she didn't even object to having her blood drawn once again.

Within moments, Mark arrived, asking if the lab had been there yet. I said yes and he continued on by saying. "Matthew, now it's much too early to make any kind of a diagnosis. We need more tests, tests that I couldn't run in my office. What I do know is her blood work didn't look right. Now, just to make certain we haven't made a mistake or overlooked something in the preliminary lab work up in my office, I want to run a few more tests here in the hospital for verification, analyze any variables that may be present—then we'll know more, and be able to pinpoint what we need to do to get Abby started on the road to recovery. Now, Matthew, listen to your doctor; go down to the cafeteria have something to eat, have a cup of coffee, try and relax and I will come find you as soon as we know more. I've placed a stat order on her test so it won't be long, I promise. Okay? Abby will be just fine, as soon as we know what bug she's picked-up. We'll know then just how to treat her. Don't worry. I'll be down soon."

I made my way down to the cafeteria as Mark suggested, had a cup of coffee, but couldn't even think of eating anything. I didn't know what was wrong, but I did know that my daughter was sick, really sick. I also knew Mark well enough to know that he, too, was as worried as I was. Time just seemed to drag by, thirty minutes became an hour; an hour became two. The longer I sat the louder my mind talk became. I prayed, and asked for patience—patience has never been my better virtue where Abby was concerned. I knew that God gives us a sound mind, a mind of understanding. However, I didn't understand what was happening to my daughter.

At 7:30 P.M., Dr. Jenkins finally walked into the cafeteria with another doctor by his side. Even before the introductions I apparently began to ask questions, seemingly without interruption, Mark explained to me later.

"Matthew, this is Dr. Ronne, I brought him in to consult with me concerning Abby's blood work," said Dr. Jenkins.

We shook hands, sat down, as Dr. Ronne continued; he said he was a specialist in the treatment of pediatric-adolescent diseases. He informed me that most of the tests that had been ordered came back, yet, out of concern he ordered a series work up of blood cultures that wouldn't be completed for several days. He went on to say that Abby would have to remain at the hospital under close supervision until they knew exactly what caused her infection.

"Matthew, a blood culture is a laboratory test to detect infections within the blood, identifying such entities as bacteria or fungi which normally aren't there. What I suspect in Abby's case is an abnormalcy called bacteremia, a serious condition, which can weaken the entire immune system. Once the cultures are back we'll know exactly how to treat your daughter," Dr. Ronne said.

He asked the customary questions concerning Abby's general health, made a few notes in his little overstuffed black jotter and said that he would be in touch as soon as he knew more. Dr. Ronne was a rather tall, lanky man standing somewhere around six feet tall, having long slender limbs, weighing every bit of two hundred fifty pounds, I would guess. He looked to be in his late sixties, and I thought how his mere physical stature demanded respect. I know his knees must have touched the bottom of the tabletop where we were sitting—he had to be extremely uncomfortable. As he pushed himself away from the table, trying to untangle his long legs from beneath his chair, I started to ask him yet another question. Mark, somehow anticipating my query, reached over the table, placed his hand on my forearm and, with a befuddled facial expression, gently squeezed my arm as if to say, let's wait.

"Mark," I asked, "just what kind of a specialist is Dr. Ronne?"

Mark responded by saying, "Matthew, I've known Robert Ronne since medical school. Believe me; he is one of the best in the country.

Honestly, at this time, we don't know exactly what's wrong with Abby. Right now all we can do is keep her from becoming any more dehydrated than she already is. Her blood chemistries are way out of line, which is a major concern—that's the reason I called Dr. Ronne in to consult. He specializes in this sort of thing. To answer your question, Robert is a metastasis platelet specialist. In laymen's terms, he deals with childhood blood disorders. Now, don't go jumping to conclusions. It might be something quite simple to treat. As your physician, rest assured we will direct all of our energies to making Abby well. As your friend, remember, I'm here for you, too. Let's not worry about anything unless we have to.

Now…go see your daughter; she been admitted to 721, she should be all settled in by now. Give her a big hug and a kiss—but don't stay to long, she needs plenty of bed rest. I ordered a mild sedative to make her sleep."

When I reached the seventh floor I asked a nurse at the nurse's station to direct me to room 721.

"I can do better than that," the nurse responded, "give me a moment or two, then we can walk down there together. I was just familiarizing myself with the paperwork for a new patient who was just admitted and, as luck would have it, my new patient just happens to be a little girl named Abby. If I were to wager, I'd bet that she belongs to you and your name must be Mr. Anderson, Abby's dad. Am I correct?"

I nodded my head as if to say yes.

"Let me introduce myself; I'm LaDonna Kingsford, the charge nurse on this shift at least for today, that is. For the most part, I generally float wherever I'm needed; normally I'm not assigned to this wing. Today I'm just covering for someone who needed off and, apparently, I was the only designated volunteer they could find," she snickered.

Walking around from behind the U-shaped desk module, she replaced a couple of charts into slotted channels hung on the wall, gesturing for me to follow her down a hallway where I was to find Abby's room.

Upon entering room 721, I certainly wasn't prepared for what I was to find. Abby was indeed fast asleep as Mark implied she might be. To my dismay, I found two intravenous tubes—one out of each arm, leading to bottled solutions suspended directly above the head of her bed. One bottle read *D5W*, a solution of dextrose and water, the other was hand-labeled with writing that I was not able to decipher. The outsides of her little hands were black and blue from needle pricks camouflaged with a copper-colored stain of betadine antiseptic.

As I watched her lying there, my heart broke into a million pieces. Mentally, I fell to my knees and asked God for a special blessing upon my daughter. I prayed as hard as I knew how, asking for strength, not only for my daughter—but for me as well. I knew she was sick…but had no idea how very ill she would soon become.

That night I fell asleep leaning against Abby's bed, my hands clasped as if still in prayer. The next morning, around 5:00 AM, I was awakened when the morning nurse came in to check on Abby's condition. It was LaDonna once again. Little did I know how significant she would eventually become to both Abby and me.

"Having to work a double shift?" I asked.

She responded by saying, "Whoever makes out the floor schedule on this ward needs to have a long talk with the nurse who was scheduled as my replacement last night. Whoever was supposed to be here for the midnight shift just never showed up, as you can see. It won't be long until the morning shift arrives. Until then, I'm all you got, fella. Can't let the patients suffer now, can we."

She walked out of the room, only to return mere seconds later, handing me a cup of coffee and asked if I took anything in it. I shook my head no and she proceeded to take Abby's temperature. As she looked at her watch, counting the pulse beats from Abby's wrist, she looked up and smiled, as if to say everything was just fine.

She didn't say another word, made a few notations in Abby's chart and left. Ten minutes or so must have gone by when she stuck her head back in the room, handing me a damp face cloth and a small bottle of Visine, along with a little complimentary travel kit consisting of a toothbrush, toothpaste, mouth wash and a comb. Her thoughtfulness allowed me the opportunity to refresh myself since I hadn't been home to pack a few things for myself.

"Mr. Anderson," she whispered, "this might make you feel better. The doctors will soon be making their rounds; actually Dr. Ronne has already been here once, must have been a little after 4:00 AM, he said he would be back later on this morning, wanting to check in with the lab first. He saw that you and Abby were asleep and said he saw no reason to wake you. I like working with Dr. Ronne, he really cares about his patients and it never surprises me when he shows up at all hours of the day and night."

I was frightened. The unknown has a way of escalating fear. I had just enough time to wash my face when Dr. Jenkins walked in.

"Matthew" he said, "How our girl doing? The nurse's notes indicate that she slept throughout the night. They also said that you didn't leave her side not for a minute. Did you get any sleep? Don't be surprised if your back doesn't stiffen up later today from sleeping hunched over the corner of Abby's bed."

"I'm okay," I answered. "Do we know anything yet? Have any of the tests come back from the lab?"

"Look Matthew, doctors really can't walk on water, we don't have supernatural powers or magical crystal balls giving us all of the answers. All we can do is make educated conjecture and develop a treatment plan. Sometimes it works, sometimes it doesn't. In Abby's case, Dr. Ronne and I concur that until all of the tests are in confirming a suspected pathogen, it would only be speculation on our part and neither one of us believes in playing God. So for now we just have to wait. I know it's hard, Matthew, but it doesn't do anyone any good to fret or worry needlessly. Don't you agree?" Mark said.

At that moment Mark's beeper went off. He looked at the number and made a call. The only remark he made was, "That's good; I will bring Mr. Anderson with me."

Mark told me that Abby would, in all likelihood, remain in a semi-hypnotic twilight sleep falling in and out of slumber, explaining that he had written a standing order for a mild tranquilizer to ensure, not only complete rest, but to forestall any apprehension and panic attacks she would naturally be feeling.

"Let's go, Matthew; Dr. Ronne is waiting for us in the conference room," he said.

As we entered the conference room, Dr. Ronne was pouring himself a cup of tea and asked if we would join him. Both Mark and I declined with a no thank you.

"Mr. Anderson," Dr. Ronne uttered, "please sit down. One of the tests came back, confirming a fear I had. Like I said, there are still several cultures that haven't come back. The one that did, however, provided me with the confirmation as to what we are facing—which will allow us to begin treatment immediately. Mr. Anderson, do you mind if I call you Matthew?"

I responded, "No, not at all, please do."

He continued, "Matthew, your daughter, Abby, I'm sorry to say has developed a condition known as acute lymphocytic leukemia; this has been reconfirmed without any doubt. This disease is characterized by an abnormal cell growth, which replicates itself over and over, producing an excessive amount of leukocytes or white blood cells in her body. You know, the disease commonly referred to as leukemia. To be blunt, what we know about this disease can be placed in a thimble; researchers are continuously learning more about this devastating disease. Still, we haven't the faintest idea as to why certain blood cells expand, invading good healthy tissue and adjacent cells. There are various levels and stages, each requiring a different course of treatment. In Abby's case, I'm a bit puzzled as to why her symptoms remained dormant until now. When the results are back, the remaining tests should give us some insight.

"As much as we would like to think that medicine is an exact science, it isn't. Matthew, the science of medicine is improving each second of the day, cures are becoming found, progress is being made in areas we only dreamed of, despite anything to the contrary— medicine is still, at times, nothing less than a process of hypothesizing, conjecture and theorizing from what facts we know, and then formulating a strategic approach—that's what medicine really is.

"Matthew, one more thing that I dread telling you—but I must be honest. In your daughter's case I'm sorry to say that when this particular type of leukemia has progressed to the point we have just found in Abby's present phase of cell division, it is with certainty…always malignant and, within an indefinite timeframe, fatal."

"Are you certain? What if we ran more tests, there's got to be more tests. What if somebody made a mistake in the lab? Are you really certain?" I questioned as tears began to roll down my cheeks.

"Yes, very certain," Dr. Ronne remarked, continuing on to say, "We'll know more as time progresses. At this advanced stage, all we can do is hit the disease with an aggressive regiment of different therapies. There are also several medications that we can try, based upon tolerance, and hope that it will…well, prolong her life. The procedures of treatment dealing with acute lymphocytic leukemia are problematic because it worsens quickly. It is the most common type of leukemia that we have found in young children.

"Now, for whatever good news there is; sometimes—not all the time, once we have found the right level of treatment, the disease has been known to regress, or remit. Now, this doesn't mean that it goes away. It just means it goes into hiding, so to speak. The patient gets better and sometimes the symptoms disappear. I have known patients who were in remission for years before the final stages took their toll. I know that you have many questions; regretfully, I'm sorry—I must leave. Dr. Jenkins will explain a normal course of treatment. Urgency is of the utmost concern at this point of time to begin Abby's treatment. I would like to have her scheduled for her first dose of radiation in the morning. As soon as I see how Abby is responding; I will then be able to update you as to my medical prognosis. I'm sorry, Matthew."

I was in a state of shock. I couldn't say a word. Mark sat with me for well over an hour, and held me as I cried. I can't explain what was in my heart and mind. The pain was so real, so devastating. With all of my might I tried to pray, but couldn't. I knew God was with me— I could feel his presence, his warmth, but couldn't reach him in prayer. Having lost both of my parents, my loving wife and now my only child, I can only believe that what I was feeling at that exact moment was my allotted share of the cross that Christ suffered and bore for me. It seemed like hours had passed by before I could ask Mark…*Now what?*

"Mark, I'm going to need your help. What can I say to Abby? She's just a child—her life has yet to begin. How can I expect her to understand when I can't? What words can I possibly use to…tell my daughter she's dying?" I asked.

Mark looked at me and said, "Matthew, God will help you find the right words when the time is right. It isn't absolutely necessary to fully explain everything to her right away; we can give it a few days. I'll write a note in her chart indicating that she has not been told, advising everyone on the staff to refrain from saying anything to her for the foreseeable future. Whatever you do, don't look at her with pity, but with a respect for what is yet to come. I know you, Matthew, and I know you can handle this."

After I pulled myself together I returned to Abby's room; Dr. Jenkins was right—she was sound asleep. I sat there by her bedside thinking the most horrendous of thoughts, weeping as if I were a child, hoping she wouldn't notice that my eyes were red from crying when she awoke. When she did awake I was surprised to find her in rather good spirits; still not her typical self, she was indifferently quiet as if her soul found solitude in the sanctum of the medication. Her only comment was asking, "Daddy, what's wrong with me?"

Just as I began to search for words to give her some sort of explanation, an orderly arrived with a lite breakfast tray of high protein foods. "After you finish your breakfast," he commented, "Amy—your floor nurse today, will be in to get you ready for Dr. Norton."

"They are going to give me more test, aren't they?" she asked.

Knowing that she hadn't any idea as to what was occurring, I dug my heels in and proceeded to tell her just how very sick she really was. Abby had such a literal mind I knew I had to be extremely careful. It's one thing to explain illness and death to a child her age;

then again, it is entirely something different to explain that same impending death is meant to be her own.

I have never hidden my feeling from Abby; I have never felt that by allowing her to see my emotional side, made me less masculine or clouded her image of me as her father. I can't count the times she handed me a Kleenex while we were watching a heart wrenching movie on Lifetime Television or even on the History Channel, when we witnessed the slaughtering of hundreds of baby seals.

I decided to be just as honest as I could; justifying what I have always taught her—that truth would always be foremost in our relationship. I also felt that by delaying any explanation it would only complicate matters further.

As soon as Abby drifted off once again, I went to the nurse's station and spoke with Mark over the telephone, advising him as to my decision. His only comment was that it might be helpful if one of the nurses were present when I spoke with Abby. As luck would have it, LaDonna was still on the floor and I asked if she would be so kind as to help me explain the unexplainable to Abby. I had little doubt she would refuse. We both returned to Abby's room where LaDonna ever so gently woke her by stroking her forehead and, in a whispering tone, called her by name. LaDonna sat on the side of her bed and the two of them spoke as if they were long lost friends.

"Hey, Dad, why don't you give us a few minutes alone? I think the gift shop is opened now and I just know you would love to go down there and find me a new teddy bear or something," LaDonna said.

I took her cue and did, in fact, go to the gift shop, returning with a doll, for lack of a better description. Actually, it was stuffed figurine of an angel holding a small kitten. I wasn't gone for more than twenty minutes or so. During that time, LaDonna had helped Abby bathe and change into a clean set of pajamas.

"Abby," LaDonna said, "your dad needs to talk with you, and I'm going to be right outside the door if you should need me. Okay?"

"Sweetheart," I said, "earlier you wanted to know if the doctors knew what was wrong and why you are feeling so sick. Well, I met with them a little while ago and they explained everything to me.

Now it's my turn to explain everything to you so we can get started making you feel better. I know you have heard the word cancer before. Let's talk about that for a minute. Cancer is a disease where the cells in your body grow abnormally.

Do you remember last year in your second grade class when Ms. Browning showed you a model of a human body and explained that our bodies are made up of different kinds of cells? She told you that there are red blood cells that carry oxygen in your blood and white blood cells that help you fight off infections, she even told you about the blood platelets that help your blood to coagulate when you cut yourself. Well, in your case, the cells in your body are making you sick by the way they're growing. They're not really working like they should. Dr. Ronne is a very special doctor who only treats children who have cancer. He's called a pediatric-adolescent oncologist, and he works with Dr. Norton who is a specialist in the radiology department, and between them they are going to try and make you feel better."

"Still more tests?" she questioned.

I didn't have the heart to give her any further explanation, needing to speak with the doctors first. I remember thinking how quickly things were happening. This time yesterday afternoon we hadn't even arrived at the hospital. Four days ago Abby barely had the sniffles, let alone knew she had this dreaded disease.

Within minutes a gurney pulled into Abby's room, making way to begin her radiation treatment. I explained that one of the ways Dr. Norton was going to make her feel better was by using something called high-energy radiation, and not to worry because it was just like having a picture taken from the outside of her body, reassuring her she wouldn't feel a thing. I sat down in a corner chair awaiting her return, knowing they would not allow me to be with her, so all I could do was wait. I tried to think things through, questioning every moment of the past few days, recalling the last time we were together before she became ill, how she made fun of the burnt hamburgers on the grill. Behind my back she ordered pizza and didn't say a word until it was delivered. I couldn't help but chuckle to myself.

Abby had always been such a great joy amazing me with her antics constantly; I never knew what to expect from one moment to the next. She made the perfect roommate, the perfect little companion, the perfect daughter, and now my whole world was starting to fall apart. I began to feel ashamed; thinking of her as if she had already died, instead of thinking of her alive and in the present.

I really don't know how I did it, but the next day I was able to explain to Abby what Dr. Ronne had said. She held my hand as she cried, refusing to let go, eventually falling asleep. Deep down I wondered if she truly understood the long-term outcome.

The first several weeks of radiation treatments were the hardest. It was decided she needed a combination of chemotherapeutic agents to coincide with the radiation therapy, hoping that we might get a good grip on this devilish disease. Losing her hair was only a small part of the devastation she felt. The nausea and extreme vomiting forced her to expel everything she ingested.

Abby adjusted rather quickly, for the most part, enduring the never ending tests of probing and prodding. She had accepted her disease much better than I had, or could. She knew she was going to die and had accepted it with great dignity. Living with leukemia was not easy, especially for a child. Just coping with the negative side effects, having to accept how some side effects could change and alter from one treatment session to the next could be overwhelming.

Dr. Ronne had a good suggestion; he recommended that I begin writing a daily journal, penning down any concerns or questions that may arise as I thought of them. He also gave me the lecture on approved foods she may or may not have, right in front of Abby to forestall any concerns in the future.

"Matthew," Dr. Ronne said, "be prepared, sooner or later your little angel will try and convince you to sneak in a cheeseburger or maybe even a pizza. If and when she does, you have to stand firm, be strong and resist her charms, not allowing even the slightest variance from her regiment, regardless of how much she may plead. Keep in mind it is only in her best interest that we not allow any deviation from approved foods, no exceptions. Abby's diet was designed for a specific medical purpose, allotting precise amounts of nourishment to allow her to maintain her ideal medical weight with just enough calories and proteins to maintain her strength to facilitate therapy.

"Matthew, it's extremely important for Abby's wellness to follow what I know seems to be severe and overly restrictive. Nutrients are essential to children like Abby fighting and struggling daily just to cope with cancer; maintaining the correct protein levels, balancing carbohydrates and fat consumption, extra fluid intake to prevent dehydration and constantly adjusting each area as need be. Robert also explained that by knowing exactly what she has eaten will allow us to be able to counterbalance any negative side effects of the nausea and vomiting."

# Chapter 4: Aunt Cissy

As Abby's father knowing that the time is at hand for this phase of her life to end while upholding my beliefs that her new spiritual life is about to begin, doesn't make it any easier to accept the inevitable. It sounds like a contradiction—I know, still I will hold on wanting her to remain with me for as long as humanly possible before she begins her heavenly journey.

Now…it's only a matter of time, all medical treatments and considerations have been discontinued; medically all of our options have been exhausted. Abby has received the very best of medical care available anywhere; the next few weeks will be directed to preparing her psychologically for what is yet to come.

Traditional cancer care aggressively accentuates the use of expensive high-tech medicines where hospitalization is required to control the disease when a cure is possible. Once the decision has been made that little else can be done medically, hospice is quite the answer for whatever remaining time there may be.

Hospice care emphasizes comfort lessen the intensity of anxieties and fears permitting persons to live as pain-free and comfortable as possible in their own homes or in hospice centers supporting the concept that everyone has a right to die with dignity. The focus of hospice is on 'compassion not curing' thereby allowing patients to take a final reprieve from the regimented structure of treatment while still ambulatory before becoming bed ridden.

End-of-life care is as much for the surviving family members as it is for the patients themselves.

This past week Abby was transferred from the oncology ward to the hospice wing. At first the move had been traumatic; she had developed so many attachments to the nursing staff, yet when she saw that all of her friends—the doctor's, the nurses and support technicians all came to visit, she settled down and reconciled herself to her new surroundings. I have left the decision to Abby as to what she wants, to return to our home or to remain in the hospice wing. Either way it was her call knowing the time frame to be short. Abby has accepted her fate far better than I have; I just want to hold her in my arms and wake up from this terrible nightmare.

The director of the hospice was a mature woman by the name of Mrs. Webster. She never used her last name, everyone simply referred to her as "Aunt Cissy." Aunt Cissy stood a bit less than five feet somewhat portly and robust. Her hair was a platinum shade of gray always worn in a bun to the back of her head, traditional in the way women wore their hair in the early forties. Her Ben Franklin style bifocals only enhanced her rather rosy red cheeks, which held a smile more times than not.

At first meeting one couldn't help but think of one's own grandmother. Abby's maternal-grandmother dies eleven months ago at age ninety-two, and having neither set of grandparents alive today Abby couldn't help but look to Aunt Cissy as a surrogate.

Cissy Webster was an extremely educated woman. Not only did she hold a Ph.D. in public health nursing but in several other doctoral disciplines as well; Doctor of Developmental Cognitive Psychology, Doctorate of Education and a Doctorate of Philosophy. The only time I had ever seen the laureate of doctor used was on the wall in the inner sanctum of her office, a place of inviolable privacy. She was insistent on not allowing anyone to call her doctor. Unless you were privileged enough to be invited into the inner retreat; you would have no idea of her many accolades, certificates and awards she had received over her many years of service. There was no pretense where Aunty Cissy was concerned; her name plate on her office door simply read…Aunt Cissy, Hospice Director.

Aunt Cissy's mere presence could change the night into day. She had a way of making everything just seem better, but without the chocolate chip cookies and cocoa. She not only gave hope and encouragement to the patients of the hospice, but addressed the needs of the surviving family members, making it a point to spend quality time daily with each room within her wing. If ever a living person deserved to be canonized, hands down—it would be the endearing soul known simply as Aunt Cissy.

Abby was beginning to have restless nights, sleeping very little. She told me that her pain was manageable but it was the reoccurring dreams that she found unpleasant.

"Daddy, I'm afraid to go to sleep. When I do I have the same dream, and in my dream I see myself with lots of people standing all around me," she said.

"Are the people standing around you in your dream, people you know?" I asked.

"I can't tell," Abby replied, "they never say or do anything. They just stand there…leaning over me. I can't really see their faces but I know they are staring down at me. It's really kinda scary and weird, Dad. And when I do wake up I can't remember anything about my dream except for the people standing over me and having a strange feeling as if I was weightless walking on a cloud," Abby said.

I told her not to worry saying that it was probably one of the side effects of her pain management medication; Abby seemed to accept my explanation, she reached out for my hand, closed her eyes and within minutes she was fast asleep.

One day during Aunt Cissy's visit, I casually mentioned Abby's restless nights, Aunt Cissy just nodded her head as if to say she understood. Before leaving Abby's room to make her rounds, Aunt Cissy leaned-over and whispered something in Abby's ear. On her way out the door, she patted Abby on the leg and said with a big smile on her face, "Remember child…God loves you, your daddy loves you and I love you. That's all the love you will ever need. Darling, when you have your bath this afternoon, send your dad to my office to have a cup of my special tea. He looks like he could use a cup, don't you agree. Got to go for now, be back later—adios, adieu, and sayonara."

After she left I asked Abby what Aunt Cissy had whispered in her ear. "Oh nothing—just some girl talk, Daddy," Abby replied.

I knew that Abby needed a certain amount of privacy, being an over protective father doesn't help either. I struggle constantly to remember that she's not the child she used to be and if she wanted me to know what Aunt Cissy had said, she would have told me.

That afternoon shortly after lunch, Abby decided that she wanted a brief nap before allowing LaDonna to bathe her. Her strength was dwindling away requiring additional cat-naps throughout her waking day suspending the conscious world around her; the fatigue by itself has taken its toll, lessening her endurance to fight-off the despondency and depression which only LaDonna had a way of dealing with. Regardless of Abby's sullenness, LaDonna always seems to know just what Abby needed to change her disposition; sometimes as simple as merely the touch of her hand; it was LaDonna who directed me on the medical wing to room 721 so long ago.

When Abby transferred to the hospice annex surprisingly LaDonna transferred too, they seemed to be drawn one to another, developing a relationship far beyond that of patient and nurse.

One day by sheer accident LaDonna and I ran across one another standing in line at the cafeteria, when I relayed our chance meeting to Abby she asked me if I had ever considered marrying LaDonna. I thought how rather odd her question was, but then again—I suppose I shouldn't be surprised, considering she has always tried to play cupid wanting to match me up with one of her friend's mothers who were also single parents from either death or divorce. If my daughter told me once, she told me a thousand times long before her illness that I needed to marry, to find someone nice to spend time with; her most precious line being, "Ya know, Dad, it won't be long before I go away to college."

Well—she was right on one point, in another nine years she could very well have been in college had it not been for this setback.

I remember one instance she and a close friend from Girl Scouts, both girls just barely eight years old I recall, went so far as to orchestrate an entire evening that ended up being most remarkable. They had arranged for a complete romantic dinner for two at the local country club which included a nice bottle of wine, a gourmet meal and the most pleasant dinner companion I could have asked for. The fact that they were able to devise and create such an elaborate escapade all accomplished unbeknownst to me and the other girl's mother, made it extremely difficult to censure their efforts once we had found out just how imaginative our daughter's were. They only wanted to find a way for the two of us to meet believing that a romantic dinner would solve the dilemma of loneliness oftentimes associated with single parenthood.

The story line they used was rather ingenious and quite inventive for two little girls to even conjure up.

They pooled their allowances together and somehow convinced yet another friend of theirs for her help, asking the third girl to speak with her father who happened to be the executive chef at the country club to see if he could prepare a romantic dinner for two with the limited resources they had. Believing Abby and BettyJo to be sisters the chef asked how much money they had to spend, he told us later that he couldn't help but chuckled to himself when he found out that they only had $27.72 but was so overwhelmed by their thoughtful gesture of wanting to do something special for their parents, he agreed saying, "Tell your parents to be at the club at 7:00 P.M. Friday night, I'll have a table reserved for them and don't worry; I won't say anything to spoil your surprise. Leave it to me; I'll take care of everything. Also tell them when they arrive to ask for seating at table number 12; it's the one table I like to reserve for couples overlooking the lake—the view is spectacular. He went on to add, "Here are two individual gift certificates for dinner, one for each of your parents. Take them home and gift wrap them separately; give one to your father and the other to your mother. I bet they are going to be so surprised." The girls thanked Chef Appleton for his help and proceeded on with their game plan. The next hurdle they had to overcome was how then to give the certificates to both respective parents together without botching their little scheme.

Abby gave me the gift certificate and BettyJo gave Victoria her certificate telling both of us—independent from one another, that they had purchased the certificates for a special 'parent's night out' at the country club apparently only held on Friday nights.

"Dad," Abby said, "I have a surprise for you," handing me her gift wrapped envelop, "You work so hard and you do everything for me, I just wanted to give you something that's kinda special ya know, just to say I love you. I even called Mrs. Clark to come over and stay with me, remember when she said that the next time she baby sat with me…hey, I just thought of something—why do they call it baby sitting anyway? I'm not a baby anymore; anyway…she said that she would teach me how to make sugar cookies, and I know how much you like sugar cookies, so ya see, I won't be here alone. What do you say?"

I didn't know what to say. I felt blessed to have such a daughter as Abby so thoughtful and caring. I gave her a big hug and thanked her saying I wouldn't miss it for the world.

Having previously attended many social gatherings at the country club I knew they were constantly thinking up ways to entice new members, and knew also that their chef and club manager were really big on creating theme dinners open to the community at large to showcase their talents and efforts to increase their wedding business. I just naturally assumed that their implementing a Friday night dinner held exclusively for a parent's night out was a good idea and gave it no further thought.

I went about my week as normal and on Friday evening after Mrs. Clark arrived, I once again told Abby how impressed I was with her gift; telling her goodnight knowing she would be in bed when I returned home.

Driving over to the country club my chest was bursting with pride, I took a moment to thank God for allowing me to have such a thoughtful considerate daughter. It wasn't until I arrived walking into the foyer that I first felt something was amiss, I didn't see any other guest waiting there to be seated. When the hostess asked "Dinner for one sir," I responded as saying, "I already have reservations and was told to request table number 12."

"Right this way", she said, "Please follow me."

Walking through the packed dining room I was beginning to feel better thinking that this dinner must have been a total sellout. Across the room I could only see one vacant table left in our walking direction and sure enough it was table number 12. The hostess remarked, "Enjoy your meal," turned around and walked away.

I sat down and within moments the sommelier approached me saying, "Sir—I hope you enjoy this particular vintage," displaying a bottle of Cotes de Provence, a rather expensive wine—saying, "It was chosen by the chef to compliment the dinner he is preparing for you." He opened the bottle and having gone through the ritual of pouring just a taste in the wine glass allowing me the opportunity to sniff the bouquet, asking "Do you find it acceptable?" I responded by simply saying "Thank you."

"Well then, may you have a pleasant evening, bon appetit," he added.

To make a long story short, Victoria and I having been thrust together compared notes on how our daughter's manipulated the two of us along the Chef Appleton, still we enjoyed a very pleasant evening once the initial shock and embarrassment worn off. Since Victoria and I could find no dishonesty or falsehood, in act or speech from either one of the girls, we decided to overlook their shenanigan omission and turn the tables on them agreeing that once we returned home neither she nor I would comment one way or another of our chance meeting. We both knew that our remaining silent to our prearranged rendezvous would drive the girls crazy; considering that they did have the best of intentions taking into account, they are just eight years old.

Each day LaDonna would come and give Abby her bath, even on the days she was scheduled off. LaDonna was beginning to spend as much time with Abby as I did. Abby became so attached to LaDonna that she even refused help from me at times. I too found myself looking forward to LaDonna's visits each day, anticipating the time of her arrival with a sense of excitement. She spent quality time with Abby, female time that I as her father could not give, affording me a little time away. I prayed for God to forgive me; I know it doesn't sound right, but I'm only human and need time to recoup my own composure, to regain my strength in order to reinforce strength for

Abby. As much as I was beginning to enjoy LaDonna's company I felt as if I needed time away from her as well.

Each day I knew I could count on a good hour or so for Abby to have her bath and body massage. God knows how much I valued LaDonna's companionship not only for Abby's benefit but for mine as well. I have become rather close to LaDonna thinking of her afar from being a caregiver, however taking special care to maintain a certain amount of distance wanting to keep our relationship platonic. I have no doubt that LaDonna loves Abby as any mother would love her own child. Although single and having never been married, naturally LaDonna never had children of her own. Her devotion to both Abby has been a Godsend, teaching by example that love is not only a state of mind but a state of the heart as well.

With the rapid decline of Abby's condition it became obvious that to return to our home would definitely not be in her best interest since now she required around the clock nursing care. The nurses and hospice workers were so diligent, taking care that Abby was turned frequently to assure against decubitus ulcers and seeing to her every need. For the most part, Abby's upper torso was propped up at an incline lying flat on her back being much too weak to turn over on her side by herself; luckily she has retained the use of her hands and arms for simple movement such as turning the page of a book or magazine.

Abby's moods became so obstinate and insistent about so many things. Then again, who could blame her? She demanded that LaDonna feed her the noon meal, no-one else, just LaDonna. As for her breakfast and dinner meals, she only wanted her daddy to feed her.

She often refused all other assistance including help from even Aunt Cissy.

There were times I became annoyed, felt exasperated and frustrated with her attitude. Nonetheless, I always kept it to myself. All it took was one look at her baby blue eyes and the pain they held, and then I realized that she was doing the best she could. I don't think she knew or realized how exacting, intense and subdued we had all become. All she knew was love and the attachments that came with it.

Whenever I felt abused, I displaced it as being tired and exhausted. God knows my heart and soul I thought to myself he wouldn't hold it against me for feeling maltreated. Several months ago Dr. Jenkins insisted that I start taking vitamin B12 shots, to increase my stamina and endurance, now I am glad he did.

When LaDonna arrived to give Abby her bath, Abby make it a point to remind me to go see Aunt Cissy. In a somewhat sarcastic pre-teen voice, she said "not that it's any of my business or anything—but, don't forget you need to go see Aunt Cissy. I think she wants to talk with you away from me. I mean…how many times—like never, has she ever asked you to come to tea anyway." I realized it was her way of turning the tables around on me, scolding me in her own little way for asking her about her conversation with Aunt Cissy that very morning. With a Cheshire cat grin upon her face she motioned me out of the room.

When I reached Aunt Cissy's office her secretary told me to go right in. Aunt Cissy was on the telephone but gestured that I come in and sit down. She put her hand on the mouth piece and in an undertone said she would only be a minute. She finished her call, got up from behind her desk walking around a side credenza adjacent to her desk and started to make us a cup of hot tea.

"None for me thank you," I said.

"Oh you must," she replied, "I told Abby that you needed a cup of my special tea, and you can't make me out to be a liar. Now can you?"

"In that case," I said, "How can I refuse? I would be delighted to share a cup of tea with you."

"Matthew," she said, "I'm interested and want to know more about Abby's dreams, I didn't want to say anything about them in front of her to give them more concern. Other than what you have already told me, did she say anything else to you? Have they been reoccurring and if so with what frequency?"

I said, "Aunt Cissy, you know as much as I do. Abby said that she didn't recognize anyone or have any idea where she was. She only said that a group of people were just standing over her as she slept. Abby had only mentioned having this particular dream within the last couple of days. The only thing I can recall that I neglected to mention was, she said that there was a young beautiful woman with long blond hair wearing a white dress standing in the center of the crowd. Other than that—I can't think of nothing else."

Aunt Cissy just stood there without saying a word. The look on her face was solemn and earnest. She then questioned, "Has she said anything about variance or variety within her dreams? Is there always the same number of people present? Is everyone present dressed in white? Has she mentioned anything about luminous color or bright lights? Look Matthew; think hard, it's very important.

Let me explain it this way. I have been the director of this hospice for almost twelve years and have seen my share of the unexplainable. This morning in my presence, you reassured Abby that her dreams were the result of the medication she is on. Visualized fantasy I think you called it, a kind of an imaginary or hallucinatory illusion caused by her failed nervous system and drug therapy. Then you looked at me and wanted me to agree with you to comfort Abby. If you recall, I didn't say anything one way or the other.

"Matthew, I'm sorry…but you're wrong. Now don't say anything, just listen. I know you're a deeply religious man and have raised Abby as a single father with the same standards. I know you have your beliefs, but don't forget that Abby has her too. Abby may still be a child chronologically but she is as grownup as any adult facing the same set of circumstances. Oftentimes, family members of someone who is terminally ill will associate certain experiences like Abby is having, as being the result of treatments and medication. Well, some research studies have shown that simply isn't the case."

"I don't understand what you're saying. Are you telling me that my daughter's dreams are real?" I asked.

"No—what I'm saying Matthew," she said "is that in all my years of caring for the dying, God has blessed me. I have given support both medically and emotionally and in return God has allowed me to share the death experience. I have devoted my life to the care and comfort for those who are about to cross over from what we call life, into that uncharted area known as the death process. Some people, how many we simply can't say as of yet, who are about to make this so-called death journey have had similar dreams to what Abby is having.

"Now, Matthew, I know this may be a bit hard to understand, as scientist we are learning more and more about the immensity of God's plan, especially where death and dying are concerned. I have reason to believe that death is indeed the link between the natural phenomenon of religious truth leading to the immortality of mankind's soul. Believe me Matthew, I'm not taking God out of this equation, on the contrary, I'm supporting that God for whatever his reasoning, has allowed some people to have a glimpse into death just before they are about to cross over. This isn't science fiction but fact I'm stating. Abby dreams may be an indication that she too is about ready to let go of her mortal body. I believe it to be one of the final stages of preparation before passing through the veil-of-life that God placed upon our eyes before we were born."

"Aunt Cissy, I have no doubt that God is awaiting Abby's return. I have a hard time accepting the idea that Abby has given up hope and is ready and willing to let go. She has hung-on so…and well, she is still here. From everything that I have ever heard or read some people who are about to die supposedly see a bright light and walk towards it. Don't they?" I said.

"Matthew, stop and think for a moment," Aunt Cissy said, "no one has ever died and returned to talk about it. What you're referring to is called a *near death experience*. Personally, I don't believe is such things. Once a mortal person has given up its soul, I find it difficult to believe that our Father in Heaven would allow them to return to their mortal state. However what I'm talking about is what I refer to as an *eternal perceptual vision*.

"When someone is experiencing an 'eternal perceptual vision', it has been described as a drifting in and out of a cognitive state into a peaceful serene splendor, floating in and out of consciousness—a condition which we the living can't begin to comprehend. They haven't died, but have been given a glimpse of life on the other side.

"I have had hospice patients tell me that they have even seen members of their immediate families who had died years previous.

Out of all of the reports that I have heard or researched, I have only found one unvarying constant, the presence of 'Guardian Angels.' After all, if angel's are spirit messengers from God sent to those who are to receive his salvation; does it not stand to reason that they too will also be present for the crossing over into immortality?

"I had one patient explain it to me this way, he said, 'Jesus Christ used metaphorical teaching; parables to teach, instruct and enlighten. He did so knowing that those who had reached a state of awareness would understand his message. When a dying person is experiencing an eternal perceptual vision they are being guided slowly into the spirit realm without Satan's fear of death standing in the way. You could also look at it as if God takes us each by the hand and escorts us through the valley of death with His entourage of angels. I'm really drawn to like this explanation.'"

I sat there in total awe and confusion. What Aunt Cissy was suggesting was far beyond my reasoning of comprehension. I have always believed in God, in angels and life everlasting. I have always believed that we as human beings do not have the capacity or ability to fully understand the death process leading into immortality, accepting on faith indisputability that we each will return to our Father in Heaven, but to accept this *EPV* that Aunt Cissy is suggesting, well, I just don't know. And up until now never gave it much thought.

Aunt Cissy looked at me and said, "It's okay not to believe in what I'm telling you. I just want you to think about it. What I am talking about is something that we couldn't change even if we wanted to. It's God's plan. Look, remember back as a young student when your teacher was trying to instruct you in advanced mathematics. You thought it was hard at first because you did not understand the basic concepts. What we each cannot understand, we each cannot perceive. What you're feeling now is the unknown, there are certain things in life that God did not intent for mankind to understand. Each of us must accept on faith that God has his reasons for the way the world was created, and the way it runs. This includes the death process too. I know we can agree that death is nothing more that the continuation and extension of life everlasting in God's presence. It's natural not to accept the death process. God intended it to be that way. Haven't you ever heard that the worst day in heaven would be far better than the very best days here on earth. If mankind really understood the death process and put aside the fears of the unknown, there would be suicides left and right. People would be taking their own life just to be in the presence of the Heavenly Father.

"God, in his ultimate wisdom, knew that mankind could not handle certain concepts and ideas; he knew mankind would place their wants and desires before his will.'

"Matthew—each of us here on earth has a specific unique purpose assigned by God himself. God in his all knowing knew that we would not accomplish our tasks if we as mankind truly understood death. That is the reason he placed a veil before our eyes. There are however certain times that God will allow us to see through the veil, and then only for specific purposes. Has not God taken care of you and Abby by providing for all of your needs? Hasn't he always been there whenever you needed him? Do you honestly think that LaDonna came into your life simply by chance? Matthew, one last thing I want you to think about—doesn't the New Testament state, I believe in Matthew 28 where Jesus said, 'I will be with you always even until the end.' Do we not agree that since God provides for the living, does it not stand to reason that he also guides and provides for the dying?"

I looked at Aunt Cissy with tears in my eyes and said, "I guess I never looked at it that way."

I picked up the cup of tea that Aunt Cissy had prepared for me; taking a sip realizing that it had turned cold. My conversation with Aunt Cissy had been so intense I forgot all about it sitting before me. Aunt Cissy looked at me and asked if I was okay, my eyes had begun to tear-up as I felt a cold chill running up my spine.

In the short time that I have known Aunt Cissy, I have grown so fond of her. Not only do I respect her as a person, I respect the caring she feels for each one of her hospice patients, and even more so I respect the knowledge she holds for sacred providence.

I thanked her for her time and asked if we could meet again. I told her that I did not discount anything that she had said; only that I needed some time to reflect and deliberate within my own mind.

When I got back to Abby's room, LaDonna was still with her. As I entered the room their muffled laughter turned to whispers. Hearing Abby laugh was a joyous sound I rarely heard. I was thankful that even in the mist of all this sorrow there were times some joy could still be found. I also thought to myself that I was so grateful for LaDonna's presence.

"Look, Dad; look what LaDonna gave me," said Abby. "It's her gold angel pin that she worn on her uniform. She said that she wanted me to have it, to remind me that my guardian angel was with me always. Isn't it beautiful? Here, Dad, pin it on my sleeve. I want to be able to look at it…always."

I looked at LaDonna and thanked her for her most valued gift.

"Matthew, it isn't anything. In fact several years ago when the guardian angel pins became so popular, especially for nurses to wear on their uniforms, I gave one to each of my patients until the cost became prohibitive. The one I gave Abby was the only one I had left—it was the one I wore. There use to be a card that accompanied each pin with a little rhyming verse explaining the story behind how we each have guardian angels. I couldn't find the card, but I know that Abby understands how special her guardian angel is," LaDonna replied.

"Once again, thank you, LaDonna," I said. "Abby and I don't know what we would do without you. You're been so sweet and kind, so considerate and giving. I really don't know what to say to express our gratitude for all that you have done."

"Then don't say anything at all," said LaDonna. "It isn't necessary. Besides, if I didn't want to be a part of your…well, I am here because I choose to be. I enjoy helping and spending time with you and Abby. Matthew, would you give me a hand for a minute. I need to go down the hall and get from fresh linen. Abby tell your dad he needs to make himself useful."

"Hey, Dad; make yourself useful, go with LaDonna she needs your help," said Abby.

LaDonna leaned over and gave Abby a kiss on the cheek and said that we would be right back.

As LaDonna and I walked out the door and headed towards the end of the hallway, she turned around and said, "Look Matthew, I wanted to talk to you alone—and I prefer that Abby not hear what I have to say, that's the reason I made up the excuse needing your help. Abby loves you so; she knows what you have given up to be by her side both night and day this past year. She's not the child you believe her to be; like she says…she's almost a teenager. Anyway, she has shared a great deal with me, some of which I wanted to share with you. I know that you believe that the two of you haven't any secrets, Matthew—there are some things that she has chosen not to share with you…and I just felt that you needed to be aware of them.

"First of all, in private she has started calling me *mom* sometimes *mother;* it makes her feel good to do so—I hope you won't object. So if by chance in your presence she does call me *Mom*, please, just accept it and try not to make a fuss. Let's agree to do it for her sake, please. Matthew I'm not trying to take her mother's place, Abby never knew her mother, and apparently since you have chosen to refrain from having any kind of relationship with another woman, personally I'm glad you didn't—it only goes to show me how dedicated you are as a father. She has never had a role model nor had any female whom she could feel close to. Secondly, when she shared with me her dreams, we talked through them; and once I explained the nature of dreaming she lost her fears. Lastly, I just want you to know—well, that I am also here for you too, as well as for Abby. Okay; now I've said what I needed to say, we better get back before she starts wondering why we are taking so long."

"LaDonna—talk about being blind-sided; I had no idea, I mean I never thought about it one way or another. I can say even without giving it any thought I have no objections to her wanting to call you *Mom*. LaDonna—I know you love her as your own; it's obvious by your love and concern. I just wish I knew what else to say…"

LaDonna responded by saying, "Then don't say nothing at all, just let the moment be. In any case—I may not want to hear what you have on your mind. Matthew, you know sometimes it's better to love from afar without the risk of rejection. Now listen—we must go, Abby is waiting, and I don't want to make her suspicious."

LaDonna's remarks were totally unexpected; believing in my heart that I had not given her any reason whatsoever to think that I cared for her beyond our Christian friendship, let alone with any adoration. I must admit however that her comments did indeed make my heart secretly flutter. I've concealed my true feelings from Abby and LaDonna for so many reasons. My dear Abigail has been gone a long time now and I feel certain that she wouldn't have any qualms or misgivings of my having someone else to share my life with; however, the timing right now just stinks. I haven't the freedom to even contemplate such thoughts or synergy. Abby is and must be my only concern and to even contemplate any kind of relationship with LaDonna at this time is absolutely foolish and absurd.

It's been a long time since I felt or looked at any woman with feelings associated as being a companion or helpmate; I've never known another woman other than Abigail; she and I both felt the support and approval of the Holy Spirit in our lives, and if ever another woman should ever walk by my side that very same approval must be present. When Abigail died—part of me died, with her death and the birth of Abby, time did not allow for anything in-between, especially trying to nurture and develop any kind of a relationship with another woman.

As LaDonna and I entered Abby's room, Abby looked at me as if to say, "Right on, Dad." She raised her frail head and smiled seeing LaDonna and me standing together in the doorway. Reading between the lines; I just knew that LaDonna and Abby had formulated some roundabout plan to play cupid, I had no proof but didn't need any. Knowing that they shared girl talk, I have little doubt that perhaps even Aunt Cissy may have had a part in their little scheme. Later that day LaDonna asked me if I had noticed Abby's facial expression and wink when we returned to her room.

Knowing Abby like the back of my own hand, I knew that she has always wanted me to find someone to share my life with; now especially so, and if by chance that someone just happened to be LaDonna, even better. Abby knew that I would not handle her death very well. Knowing her mind and her way of thinking she believes that if LaDonna were a part of my life, I wouldn't face the future all alone.

The very next day when Aunt Cissy came in to see Abby, I asked her whenever she could spare a few moments; I would love to share another cup of her fine tea. She said she were free right then, give her a few minutes and we could meet in her office.

I spoke openly with Aunt Cissy as if she were my grandmother and I was there seeking her stellar advice. I told her of the dialog that LaDonna and I had the day previous relaying most of the conversation I could remember including that of how Abby came to look upon LaDonna as a mother figure, even to the point of calling her *Mom*.

At that point Aunt Cissy interrupted me saying, "Matthew, I have to ask—where have you been? Did you fall out of a tree and hurt your head causing selective amnesia? First, give me your word that you won't repeat anything I'm about to tell you. You have to promise— I will not misplace a personal trust given to me from your daughter who happens to be one of my patients, as well as one from a previous hospital employee. Now promise me that you will not say anything to either one of those girls until they themselves bring the issues up to you. And then, I would appreciate your acting deaf, dumb and blind as far as this conversation is concerned. Okay? Now do you promise?" she asked.

Several months ago long before Abby moved from the medical ward here to the hospice, LaDonna and Abby became thick as thieves you might say, even to the point of keeping you, apparently, well in the dark. It's true, LaDonna fell in love with Abby—and I ask you, how could she not. Abby has such a beautiful spirit, and she and LaDonna could easily pass for being mother and daughter. If truth be known I have personally overheard total strangers down in the cafeteria make remarks that could be construed as their being parent and child. They have the same physical characteristics, factual structure even down to the color of their hair. They look alike; they think alike and have even begun to manipulate you in the very same manner with or without your knowing.

I've also known for some time now that LaDonna was hopelessly in love with you. I'm truly amazed how you couldn't tell how she felt about you; it's obvious to everyone around here, except you that is.

And with a hint of witticism in her voice said, "And yes, I am very familiar with Abby's matchmaking. Some months ago during one of our sessions she asked me how I really felt about LaDonna. I told her I couldn't answer that simply because it wouldn't be appropriate and actually had no bearing on our session. It was at that time that she conveyed with me her true feeling about LaDonna. Shortly after that, I started conferring with LaDonna as if she were Abby's mother, not only that of her caregiver. I'm truly astonished, really I am—how it has remained such a secret this long. Knowing that you have had your head buried in the sand, I'm relatively certain that you must be unaware that LaDonna no longer works here at the hospital. Am I correct?"

"What," I exclaimed, "she doesn't work here, and I see her every day taking care of Abby as she has always done since Abby's transfer here to the hospice."

Aunt Cissy looked at me and said in a satirical sarcastic voice, "Matthew, I'm sure glad you're not my brain surgeon—you haven't the slightest idea of what's been going on all around you, actually at times you must have the cognitive perception of a gnat, really you must. Let me explain; LaDonna took a leave of absence from her nursing post on the oncology ward since the very day Abby transferred here to the hospice. Unfortunately we could not endorse a transfer for LaDonna since she did not have the requisite training background we stringently require from our staff. Had she not worked for the hospital as a register nurse we never would have allow her to take charge of Abby's medical care. Actually she did everything short of begging—no, that's not correct, in truth she did beg me for a transfer and with a heavy heart I had to explain that her transferring to the hospice was simply out of the question. All she wanted was to take care of a little girl whom she had grown to love. Initially I couldn't warrant such a request, and after much persuasion from both Abby and LaDonna, I met with the hospice board of commissioners who after great unequivocal *reductio ad absurdam*—remember your Latin Matthew, meaning to show how a negation leads to a contradiction of terms resulting in a positive, well…my oral petition must have been compelling because they so graciously granted a provisional oncology accreditation certificate for LaDonna mandating certain restrictions that you need not bother yourself with.

"The fact is, they approved LaDonna's request to give care in a nursing capacity—however, it must be done so only on a voluntary basis without pay. I'm sure that insurance indemnity standards had a lot to do with their dictates. Can you now understand how much love she holds in her heart for Abby and let's not exclude you; for her to be willing to make such a great sacrifice. So you see—she too has been living off of her savings just to be near the two of you. Abby has always known, she and LaDonna just kept it from you, and I know for a fact that they had every intention of telling you as soon as they could find the appropriate time. Believe me; any disregard or deceit for your beliefs or feelings were not done out of betrayal but rather out of love."

I sat there bewildered, knowing I must have had a blank look upon face.

"Matthew," Aunt Cissy said, "I know you have concerns, I also know without any doubt that little girl who calls you daddy has her concerns, too. I cannot stress this hard enough—it is imperative that she knows that you, too, will be alright. Your little girl is acting as mature as most adults I know. She knows how LaDonna feels about you as a man, now you may not want to accept what I am about to say; I do believe that deep down inside your soul you have feelings for LaDonna, too.

"During several of our sessions, Abby has expressed that she feels she is to blame for your not allowing another woman to share your life with. Assuredly I explained that wasn't the case. Abby's an intelligent little girl and needs to know that you're going to be okay, and has trust in LaDonna knowing she will see to it.

"In her adolescent mind she is trying ever so hard to understand the rationality that if all three of you each love the other two, why then have you not formed a family. In her mind it is about time for the two grownups to start acting as adults and admit that they do in fact love and respect one another, and I quote her saying, "they are just ripping themselves off and don't even know it."

"There isn't a father in this world who could love his daughter any more than you do, to be concerned about her well being is one thing, but, you cannot overlook your own welfare either.

"Matthew, I'm a firm believer that there are no accidents in this world. We each have free-will but have you ever stopped to think how our lives are ushered by the hands of the Holy Spirit, giving each of us direction and oftentimes a push when needed to fulfill purpose and guidance. Maybe, just maybe you should start listening to the spirit within instead of automatically thinking and responding to what you believe is your best course of action logically."

# Chapter 5: The Angels Listen In

The conversation I had with Aunt Cissy was to say the least enlightening—I truly enjoyed the philosophical elements stretching my mind and intelligence. She and I agree as to our thoughts and points of view with reference to near death experiences, however, her conceptualization of 'eternal perceptual visions' will however warrant great thought and prayer before I can makeup my mind to accept or reject that particular tenet one way or another. I am somewhat bothered by the terminology she used of 'eternal perceptual vision'; hopefully not universally coined yet, I think the name implies having visions upon our deathbed which I believe is misleading,

I think it more befitting to call it what it actually is, a *'celestial awakening'* or perhaps maybe *celestial awareness.*

Thinking of celestial beings has drawn my attention to a discussion that Abby and I had some time ago.

"Daddy, I want to talk about something and need to ask you some questions too. I'm glad you think I am old enough for you to share things with me; but right now I'm kinda confused.

"Last week when you were in the shower you had a telephone call and you told me then to take a message and that would return their call as soon as you finished. I remember his name was Mr. Motley and the only message he left was to tell you he had good news for us. He told me that he couldn't leave his number, but he would just call back. When he did call back he asked you if you believed in Jesus Christ and you said to him that you would be glad to sit-down with him and have an open Bible study if he would like. That's when you said there was silence he didn't say a word for several moments—

because you believed he didn't know how to respond to your offer; and when he did speak, you said he seemed to be tongue-tied stumbling over his words trying to figure out what to say next. You told me he apologized saying that his schedule would not allow any kind of one-on-one Bible study, but if you sent a donation to his church, he knew God would grant his angels the power to bestow countless blessing upon us as a family. I remember you even kinda snickered after you hang-up the phone.

"You explained to me that he was nothing more than just a salesperson, a telemarketer reading from a script who was supposedly representing some church you never heard of, I think you called it 'the Church for Christian Unification.'

"Dad…what I don't understand is why you just didn't tell him how you feel about God?" asked an inquisitive eight year old Abby—adding, "If the Bible tells us to go out and tell people about God and heaven and love, why didn't you just tell Mr. Motley about what we believe?"

"Sweetheart," I said, "I know you have seen people going from door to door handling out pamphlets to different churches they happen to belong to."

"Kinda like missionaries—is that what you mean?" interrupted Abby.

"Well, no—not exactly," I answered, saying, "I don't approve of the way most unsolicited groups using the name of God calling themselves missionaries; believe me they each have their own hidden agenda's, in the end asking for money by means of deception before they hang-up the telephone. Those so-called missionaries distort the gospel in so many ways saying that only their only their church is the light leading to heaven giving what sounds to be solid reasoning. Abby, there are so many people out there who are lonely, vulnerable and weak and would believe most anything, giving away what little money they may have believing that their so-called charitable gifts—will support those who are preaching the gospel to non-believers all over the world. It's sad to think that many of these people believe that the money they give will buy them a seat in heaven next to God himself. When Mr. Motley tried to tell me that God would direct his 'angels' to give us blessings the hairs on the back of my neck stood straight up. We have had talks about angels before, so I know you understand who and what they are, but for a so-called missionary to imply that angels can or will give blessings to anyone is nothing less than blasphemy. A true missionary would never ask for money, a true missionary doing the work of the Lord wants nothing more than to share the teachings found in Paul's epistles, never using the scriptures as a scare tactic generating fear, and if by chance a person decides to make a donation on their own free-will, that's great."

Abby just sat there with a blank look on her face, seeming to be more confused than ever. I continued on by saying, "Honey, as you grow older you will have a better understanding of why I believe as I do. I have always downplayed my personal beliefs when speaking of religious matters to anyone whom I don't know. I do this for several reasons; my primary reason being to avoid the possibility of provoking any anger or antagonism stemming from a possible disagreement we may have concerning dogma's in general. I have found that most people are pretty much one sided and have a tendency to overreact when someone has a belief contrary to their own.

"Can you understand now why I answered him as I had?"

"You're right, Dad, it's kinda hard now to think about it—but what about the things that he said that aren't true, you know the part about what angels can do and what happens with the money people send in, won't those people be punished or anything?" Abby asked. "Darling, tell you what, go get your Bible and let's read a couple of verses that come to mind together, well actually I'm thinking of three verses. I'm going to pour myself another cup of coffee and when you get back I want you to lookup Deuteronomy 4:2; which tells us that we should not 'add' or 'take-away' from the words in the Bible, also Proverbs 30:5; also tells us that 'every word' of God has been proven true, and lastly Revelation 22:18-19; this is the scripture where John the beloved is telling everyone who hears the words that are written in the Bible that if anyone adds anything to what is written in this book, God will add to him the kinds of trouble that this book tells about, and if anyone takes away any part of this book that tells what will happen in the future, God will take away his part from the tree of life and from the Holy City, which are told about in this book."

"Abby—it's been my experience that there are those it's sad to say, who hold religious theory and beliefs without knowing why. They simply do as their parents did without question holding on to religious principles which has been passed down generation after generation that quite possibly may be misleading. Honey, I have known people who have never read the Bible, when asked why, all they could say was it never seemed that important, besides it's old and it can't be trusted anyway.

"Abby do you remember the old man Mr. Scotch who lived down on the corner? One day when I was outside watering the lawn he walked over and asked me if I knew anyone who might be interested in buying his house. I told him I was sorry to see him leave the neighborhood and asked him where he was moving to. He said he wasn't moving out of his house because he wanted to saying that the doctors just gave him a short time to live telling him he had lung cancer. I questioned Mr. Scotch asking him if he was right with God and he told me, "You bet I am." I asked him if he would like some Bible time together hoping to ease his transition, and he said, "Nope, don't think so. I've never read the Bible, don't see any reason to start now—but I have Momma's Bible sitting on the coffee table. I'm a good person, my parents never read the Bible either and they raised me to fear God and follow the Ten Commandments and I know that they are in heaven with Jesus right now."

"Baby-girl, if only people would learn that personal growth can only come by the reading and searching of the scriptures firsthand, intended to initiate even more contemplation allowing each of us then to foster our own interpretation. Abby, think about this; how do you think Christ will respond to anyone standing before the judgment seat making excuses saying 'But Lord, I was always told, or my mother was the religious one in our family and she said, or perhaps someone else saying—I just always believed that because I just do. Another misconception I've heard is how some people have been led to believe that when we die, especially little children, God makes some of them angels.

I haven't discussed this with Abby, but her dreams though not alarming have caused me to consider that perhaps the people she sees standing up over her bed are in truth—angels. We each have our beliefs as to their existence, for me personally I have no doubt that they are ever present to assist all persons who have accepted Jesus as their Christ, living a life in accordance to God's plan of salvation. I have always believed on faith the existence of angels but when one experiences a firsthand encounter there is no doubt to God's special plan of deliverance for mankind.

As graduate students Abigail and I decided to go on a skiing trip to Vail, Colorado shortly after we were married. The condo we had rented before arriving was arranged by a rental service associated with the college, giving us a much appreciated discount for booking a bit early in the season. The ski-lifts were just becoming operational making way for the full impact of the season just weeks away. There was plenty of snow and the lodge was already crowded and bustling with energetic noisy activity. The cabin we were assigned was nestled on the side of a mountain, accessible only by foot some half-mile from the main lodge. From our assigned parking area it must have been a good 500 yards to walk down this narrowing pathway meandering back and forth leading to the entrance of the cutest cabin either one of us had ever seen. It was secluded and picturesque as if Norman Rockwell himself had created the view. It had snowed rather heavily one night covering the pathway entirely with a blanket of snow at least eight inches deep; Abigail and I found comfort in thinking how pleasant it was just to be able to sit by the fireside, read a good book and merely watch the snow fall with all of its splendor dancing to the rhythm of the wind. On the front wall of the cabin next to the main entrance was an over-sized bay picture window overlooking deep into a ravine, a beautiful majestic view but far too dangerous to venture out on without knowing the geographical layout of the land.

Just thinking about this encounter still gives me the chills. I was lost in thought—thinking on a verse I had just read in Hebrews 13 verse 2; marveling in the whole idea how wonderful it would be to be entertained by angels aware or otherwise. It was exactly 10:10 P.M. on Wednesday night when we heard a muffled knocking from the cabin's front door. We were surprised to think that anyone would even think about venturing out in this kind of snowstorm. I jumped to my feet with your mother at my side, opened the front door to find two average looking young men wearing what I considered rather light ski jackets with no head gear. I invited them in saying 'please come in out of the cold.' The taller of the two men responded by saying, "Thank you but no, we only stopped by to ask you if you knew about the love that Jesus Christ holds for you, however seeing his sacred text in your hand we can see that you do. May the blessings of the Lord be with you always." At that point they simply turned around and walked away.

Abigail and I both looked at one another dumbfounded and spoke almost in unison, saying to each other how very odd and strange—especially this late in the evening, and then their not wanting to come in from the cold knowing that the temperature was well below freezing.

It was obvious that they were missionaries; polite, well spoken and neatly dressed especially so for ski-wear. Contemplating to myself, why come this late at night? Actually what really came to mind were the different sets of young men whom I had gained a new found respect for having seen on campus at the library every so often, they too were missionaries who have given much all over the world in the service of their beliefs regardless of the seasons or weather conditions.

"Matthew," Abigail said, "It's much too bizarre, call them back; it's obvious that they are missionaries by what they said."

At that exact moment I realized that I hadn't put down my Bible when I went to answer the door; I was still holding it in my left hand using my index finger as a bookmark, that's what he must have meant saying he could see we were believers.

Within mere seconds I re-opened the front door only to find them gone. Immediately I ran to the back of the cabin opening the bedroom window which was facing upwards towards the parking area hoping I could stop them on the walking path, but with no avail, they were already out of sight. That's impossible I thought to myself, maybe they're standing at the corner of the cabin in a blind-spot running to another window only to find that I couldn't see them there either.

"Matthew," Abigail said, "Let's walk up and meet them in the parking area, it's going to take them a few minutes to remove the snow from their windshield, I'm sure we can catch them up there and ask them to return. I'll make some hot cocoa and give them a snack."

We only had to slip-on our boots and grab our coats and within, oh—three minutes or so, Abigail and I were walking out the front door only to be stopped in our foot steps, frozen by disbelief of what we found.

NOWHERE and I mean nowhere did we find footprints in the snow, not on the front porch, not up the pathway, we even walked up to the parking area thinking at least we would find furrows in the snow from automobile tires. All we found was a fresh blanket of snow, no visual sign that anyone had ever been there.

It was a feeling that I can only describe as being overwhelmed in a perplexing way, that no human explanation could come anywhere near what we had experienced.

Abigail and I must have stood there for a good twenty minutes trying to find some sort of rational explanation, but found none.

We then realized how fortunate we were to have witnessed such a miraculous phenomenon known as entertaining angels unaware.

The Bible teaches that angels are present at the time of our death assisting those who are to receive their celestial reward. They act as chaperons from this life leading to the divine presence of God. Jesus taught in the book of Matthew of his use of parables; giving way for his analogy in Luke 16 verse 22 of the Christian Bible.

The mention of angels is broad in scope and substance, in the Christian Holy Scriptures; from the first book of Genesis to the last book of the Bible, Revelation. I have personally found the mention of celestial beings in 34 books of the Christian Bible with their reference in excess of 100 times in the old testament and then again some 92 times in the new testament. One can find the mention of angels in the Quran and also the Torah, each having their own account of doctrine.

Angels in Islam are light-based creatures, created by Allah to serve and worship him. The "messenger." The "mise-en-scene" or background knowledge of angels described in Islam are very similar to the version described in the Christian Bible.

Angel's are intangible beings lacking a prescribed substance, shape or form. They are incapable of being touched or seen unless their visit requires such, and then so only in spirit form. Angels have no gender, they are asexual and do not reproduce, they are created beings of *Spirit* and are not the souls of departed human beings as we learn from reading in Psalm 148.

Their fundamental principle was designed to serve God; they can assume any form and traverse distance within the blink of an eye, this is where the illusion or misconception of having wings must have come from. However, contrary to Christian beliefs in which angels have free will, angels in Islam cannot fall from their status as a servant of God since they were made to be completely obedient and it is impossible for them to override or disobey a command from Allah. Every reference to angels in Christian writings is always adjunct to some other topic, to confirm God's message or direct an action from or about God. Knowing what I know about angels I am a firm believer that angels are everywhere and do indeed watch over us giving each of us well-defined signs of their presence, offering comfort, peace and even protection during times of need. I believe with all my heart that angels officiate in a variety of specific roles in the lives of all believers, many of which are unknown for a variety of reason known only to God.

# Chapter 6: Doubting Thomas

Just recently a dear friend whom I had lost contact over the years suddenly appeared at my front door, his name was Thomas Shaw. There was a time he and I were the best of friends throughout our high school days, and as life would have it we merely drifted apart living our lives independently. In actual fact Thomas and I never attend the same schools; I attended a parochial school for young gentlemen, Thomas on the other hand was educated in the public sector. His family life was altogether different from mine; his parents were atheist holding no religious orientation whatsoever especially loathing that of the Catholic Church. We had an agreement, a bond early-on in our friendship as young boys accepting the differences we each had and vowed by a blood oath as 'Indian Lore Blood Brothers' to walk the path of truth as we each may see it.

Having given my life to God as a young teenager I knew I had the advantage over Thomas; all I had to do was merely be myself, allowing Thomas to see by my example how a believer in Christ lives their life. Throughout the years it made no difference—his family constantly stressed agnosticism denying the existence of God with unwavering determination.

When the Vietnam War broke out I remembered Thomas dropping out of junior college his first year at mid-term enlisting in the U. S. Army. I tried to reason with him with no avail, his mind was made-up saying, 'I'm going to die someday and it might as well happen while defending my country', he said with his usual buffoonery. I felt then as I do now, my friend was more or less running away from life itself not having any direction to look towards. I recall how unhappy Thomas always seemed to be;

everything in life was always a big joke and he didn't appear to mind constantly taking one step forward and two steps back. I can't recollect exactly why we became best friends we surely didn't have anything in common except—well, I just don't know why, I suppose there were many distinguishing differences allowing each of us to be who we were. I was the physically underdeveloped studious type always wanting to please; he, on the other hand, was the perfect "Ken Doll", muscular, all-American looking, he-man type all the girls wanted to be seen with who disliked academics, always wanting to be the center of attention—the life at every party. He called me "Preppy", and I called him "Herc", short for Hercules. Somehow we seemed to compliment one another in a rather odd sort of way.

Standing in the doorway we hugged as long lost friends would do, I was anxious to hear all about his life. Calling Thomas by his nickname I said, "Herc, after all these years what brings you here, I mean it's been what sixteen—seventeen years since we spoke last?"

"Preppy, my friend, it's been closer to twenty years now," he responded. "If you only knew how much I have missed you over the years, do you remember how our parents use to say how we were joined at the hip, funny but I don't think they ever realized how much my alter-ego relied on you. Matthew, I can't tell you how often I had thought of you wondering how things turned out in your life; I hope you don't mind my barging in like this but I do need a favor. Don't worry my friend, I'm not here to put the bite on you for money or anything like that—but, say fella you really do look great, no doubt about it—time has been good to you. I heard you married Abigail King; my folks kept in touch as much as they were able, sending me copies of the hometown Gazette whenever they could. I also saw the funeral announcement when she passed-on."

"Herc, the last I heard from you—you were making a career for yourself in the military stationed somewhere overseas. Are you still in the army? Where are my manners? I just can't believe your actually here, Thomas we really don't need to stand here in the doorway like total strangers, please—please come in and sit down, let's have a cup of coffee and we can catch-up with one another," I said.

"Sounds great," he said as I ushered him through the family room down a hallway which led to the kitchen.

"Matthew to answer your question I'm no longer on active duty—actually I'm drawing a pension, I was medically discharged a year ago and it has taken me this long to build up enough courage to contact you.

"Don't be ridiculous," I said, "Thomas why not just come straight to the point? Are you in trouble or something? What is it?"

"Okay Matthew, I'll try to make an extremely long story short," Thomas said—adding, "Actually it's because of you I'm here, there I go again putting the horse before the cart."

"There you go again? I can see that you haven't changed much over the years; you're just as flighty as ever, scatterbrained and stumbling over your own two feet," I said.

At that moment Thomas stood up and showed me a sight I just couldn't believe. He lifted up his sport shirt exposing his chest turned around slowly showing me his back, where I saw the most hideous repulsive scars I could have imagined. His chest and back looked as if he had been beaten with a bullwhip tearing his skin to threads. His torso front and back had been marred and disfigured with raised areas of scar tissue.

He walked over to the counter and helped himself to another cup of coffee saying, "Matthew, please bear with me a minute, I have a hard time dealing with what I am about to tell you, the nightmares never go away. Believe me—it's not easy trying to recall the worst hell one could ever imagine and at the same time conceive of quite the opposite."

I was in a state of disbelief wondering what could have happened. Injuries like that had to be extremely painful to have left markings like those.

He began by saying, "It's been so many years since I was home, so many things have changed. I don't know how but I just knew I could trust in your helping me.

"Matthew, I've been imprisoned in my own little world even after my release from the P.O.W. camp. I was tortured as you can see from the physical scars, the war was supposedly over during the reunification in 1975, but in reality it wasn't. There were still Viet Cong guerrilla movements active for quite some time after the cease fire armistice. I was held captive for seven months as a political detainee, never knowing the exact locations having been blindfolded during each forced move.

"Let's change the subject for a minute, like I said it's sometimes hard to talk about. Tell me about that little girl of yours, what did you name her?"

I responded by saying, "Thomas—next to Abigail's memory I have the most remarkable precious little girl, her name is Abby, she'll be three years old her next birthday. Abigail and I were married for nearly 18 wonderful years; she suffered cardiac failure when Abby was born, and passed away early the next morning after giving birth. I'm learning to be okay now, the pain never goes away, I'm dealing with it—it's not easy but I have learned to cope," I said.

"Matthew, I'm sorry," said Thomas, "Your right about learning how to cope, sometimes involuntary acceptance is all you can do. Just ask me, I can tell you how coping can be a way of life as normal as catching one's breath.

"Matthew, you and Abigail made the cutest couple and everyone knew the two of you would one day be married. Sorry I wasn't there for you when you lost her. My mother told me you were teaching at Broadwater Middle School, do you like teaching? That's a silly question now isn't it, I mean duh—that's all you ever talked about when we were kids, how someday you were going to become a teacher—well, I can see you made it. A minute ago you used the word 'cope' well that's the reason I came to see you. I'm having a hard time trying to 'cope' with my life."

"What is it that you're trying to cope with exactly, those scars?" I asked.

"Well yes and no, but not exactly. I really don't know where to begin," Thomas said, "Remember when I told you I was going to enlist in the army and you tried talking me out of it. Do you remember what happened? Don't you remember we had a biggest fight ever and you said 'you hoped I wouldn't get myself killed' and I responded by telling you it was none of your business. I also said that if you really had a connection with that God of yours you better call in your markers because I might need them. You came right back at me saying that your minister at your church gave a sermon one Sunday and made the statement that 'during time of war—there are no atheists in foxholes'; I was extremely sarcastic about a lot of things, that was the day we both broke our promise about our different beliefs.

"Matthew, how I have regretted that moment, during the entire I was held captive as a P.O.W. that whole incident and the blowup we had ran over and over again in my mind. We never had a fight like that before, I regretted the way we parted back then—I mean we never even said goodbye to one another, not best wishes or good luck or anything.

"I remembered thinking that I saw tears in your eyes and how you really were my best friend thinking only of me and what was in my best interest. You were right, had I not enlisted I'm sure my life would have turned out much differently."

"Thomas—we can't beat ourselves up for what might have been, I'll be honest with you, I did pray for you every day at first, then it became only on occasion whenever I heard something on the news that prompted my thinking of you. But why are you so hang-up on the conversation we had after all these years? Even best friends have disagreements," I said.

"Let me continue; when I first entered the army during basic training I knew I made a mistake, how I had wished I would have stayed home and remained in school. After basic next came my advanced individual training with the Corp of Engineers my MOS or military occupational specialty was working as a heavy equipment operator. After A.I.T., advanced individual training, I applied to go to paratrooper's school down in Georgia, upon completion I volunteered to go to Vietnam during the height of conflict from 1964 to 1968. Before you can ask—I'll answer your next question, why did I volunteer to go with a knowing that I was walking right smack in the middle of a massive conflict? To be perfectly honest I did so for selfish reasons—the money; combat pay is a real bonus when you're making a little more than a raw recruit with E-4 pay of only $112.50 a month. That's the reason I put in for jump school—for the additional pay before putting in my papers volunteering to go to Nam.

"Something happened I can't describe, somewhere along the way I fell in love with the country, it's people and its modest uncomplicated lifestyle. I really felt a connection there unlike anything I had ever known, I always said if given the chance I could live there.

"Seven years later I had the opportunity to volunteer once again to return to Vietnam as a trade consultant downplaying our military status. We worn traditional military issued jungle clothing void of any insignias giving aid and support with re-unification efforts rebuilding their country laid waste by war. The Vietnamese are a proud people but were in dire need of experts in various construction trades to guide their rebuilding efforts primarily in road construction and secondarily the clearing off of war damaged countryside where hospitals and schools where slated to be built.

"That's where I met a Vietnamese woman by the name of 'Noi Lee.' We dated for about a year and as my luck would have it, she became pregnant—refusing to have an American baby saying she would be shunned by her people and decided she was going to have an abortion. I told 'Noi Lee' that I would take the baby and raise it myself. She refused—that was until I offered her money to allow me to have the child, and then—you won't believe this; I spent the better part of the next year in Hanoi working between administrative districts each having territorial dominion over various judicial issues, paying off appointed officials to approve my petition of adoption, they called it an administrative fee. I jumped through hoop after hoop eventually agreeing not disclose any element of the adoption for 'Noi Lee' to save face, having received her share of $15,000.00 which I had to beg, borrow and sell everything I owned including my restored 1962 Corvette back home in Indiana.

"After everything I went through you would have thought that I would have taken my new found daughter and fled the country, but I didn't. I named her 'Chi Ming.' After the adoption was finalized I still had another eight months on my enlistment, the 'JAG'—judge advocate general who helped me with the adoption recommended that I place 'Chi Ming' in the day care center on-base where she could be looked after by Americans. I decided I was going to apply for an early out and that quite possibly 'Chi Ming' and I could be stateside within six months.

"Matthew, it was never love with 'Noi Lee'—only lust; but I do love my daughter with all my being. For the first time in my life I really knew what love was, true honest benevolent love. It was the first time in my life I care about something more than I cared about myself."

"Thomas, I'm a bit confused. What is it exactly you need from me?" I asked.

"Matthew, please put up with my ramblings for just a little while longer—there's more to the story you don't understand yet. Funny how life can turn on a dime, how we both ended up as single fathers raising daughters on our own.

"Anyway, I felt pretty good about things making plans for my daughter and myself as soon as my enlistment was up. The duty officer advised me that he needed for me to head up a training session in the use of some equipment heading to Cambodia as a "T.D.Y.', temporary duty assignment, returning to my regular status as soon as I finished giving orientation and training to a group of local workers figuring five or six days max. The day care center was more than accommodating, they arranged for a sitter to watch over 'Chi Ming' until I returned. Everyone knew the great lengths I had gone through to prove and regain my parentage for my child and was totally supportive.

"Just southeast of the checkpoint leading into Cambodia as we were unloading a bull dozer an infiltrated North Vietnamese snipers bullet caught my left arm just below my shoulder, I was losing blood fast feeling weak and lightheaded yet somehow managed to rip-off my shirt using it to compress my wound trying to tie-off the artery to reduce my blood loss. Knowing it might be days before anyone would even begin to look for us, I thought to myself I didn't even have a sidearm for protection. The soldier who was with me was actually my sentry a member of the provost marshals office working as detailed security; he was killed instantly from another well placed round directly to his forehead. At that moment I just knew I was going to die, I was all alone out in the middle of nowhere and all I could think about was my child with total strangers back on the base. I remember wondering if I died what would happen to her, I knew the military would do something, but questioned what in my mind.

"I lose consciousness and to this day I still can't remember what exactly happened next. When I did wake up I was laying on a leech infested bloody table held securely down by leather straps with a cotton gag taped over my mouth. It was obvious that this was a makeshift surgical area or worst yet a place where the Viet Cong tortured prisoners. I suspected the bullet in my upper arm had been removed because of the improvised gauze wrapping around my arm in sling fashion, within days my wound became infected, septic, fowl-smelling and festering with a discharge of pus. The pain I thought was unbearable—little did I know how soon my endurance was to be tested.

"One of the Viet Cong guards spoke with a broken French and English dialect said I was being held as a political prisoner. I tried to explain every chance I had that I was a solder in the army and that the Geneva Convention forbid prisoner of war inhumane treatment, that a truce had been called and we were there to assist in rebuilding their country. 'Charlie' the VC guard kept saying, 'You no soldier—you spy, you die!' Later on, I was glad that I kept my ability to speak fluent Vietnamese to myself learning to listen very carefully to every conversation I over heard.

"There were seven of us at this particular location; three were civilians who had accepted contract work from the newly reformed government of Vietnam. One time I overheard two guards talking and heard what I believed to be the word Laos, figuring that's probably where we had been taken, but I wouldn't swear to it. We were always on the run, moving from one location to another deeper and deeper into the jungles.

"Once a day we were fed a small bowl of maggot infested rice, maybe a fish head every now and then, the only water we had was what we were able to collect from rainfall.

"Each of us was tormented emotionally and mentally. However, only two of us were physically tortured because they believed we were high ranking political spies gathering 'Intel' concerning war crimes.

"My physical abuse began almost immediately. The trauma of being captured by the enemy is one of the most devastating events psychologically, second only to physical torture that can happen to any member of the military. When 'Charlie' realized I had regained consciousness I was isolated away from my fellow prisoners placed in a small cage, barely four feet by four feet, unable to stand upright, confining like an animal. Every few hours some 'VC guard' would insert a long pole between the barbed-wires jabbing me in my shoulder asking if I was ready to sign antiwar statements they had written.

"They would say, 'Sign here—name, rank, hometown in the USA—sign you go free.'

"After my refusal the third or forth time I was bound by rope hog-tied with my hands touching my ankles where I was left for the next two days without food or water, guards urinating on me as they passed by. Some prisoners were hung upside down, others beaten until compliance and submission and then there were those who were forced to stand for hours holding a bag of sand in each hand held upright shoulder level. Matthew, if you could only imagine out of fear for your life and the lives of those around you being forced to crawl through latrine pits filled with human excrement. Prisoners were beaten with whatever 'Charlie' had in hand. Every day the same scenario took place; 'Sign here—sign here—go home.'

"On my 29th day of my internment, the torture of cutting and cauterizing my flesh began. The 'VC' were skilled in methods of inflicting pain and suffering; on one hand they could use their talents to hand carve a beautiful scenic display on a piece of scrimshaw as a work of art, on the other hand they were just as precise using a panga, a rusted machete looking knife, to inflict pain. As soon as one incision was beginning to scab over they would re-open the same cut-line only wider the second, third and so on time after time. The one area just above my left breast was cut eight times before we were rescued. The pain was excruciating hoping my mind would give way to losing consciousness each time I faced a cutting.

"Within weeks I was desperate to find a way out, seeing no escape, I cried for death to take me. I guess you could say I tried your praying Matthew, but it didn't work. I didn't believe your God would kill me even if he could—but at least it occupied my mind for a period of time. I would say, 'God if you are real—show me, take me away from the horrible place.' The only sanctuary I found was in my mind's eye losing myself to my own imagination and fantasy, thinking of better days. I thought about everything I had ever done every place I had ever seen but mostly more times than not I thought of our boyhood times together. I tried to recall if I ever saw you praying—thinking maybe I wasn't doing it right. I thought if God really did exist why he allowed such pain and anguish to continue without stopping it. I thought about the theories my parents held and how they were different from God fearing believers. I was able to question what I believed or rather what I was taught to believe objectively and honestly for the first time in my life. Each time as I traveled in and out of consciousness I would travel deeper into my own little world allowing my fear of confinement and claustrophobia to vanish.

"Somewhere around the beginning of the third month, I had already lost track of days, and I couldn't be certain how long I had been there. During the night a steady storm of violent rain had bombarded our camp when the 'VC' placed a new prisoner in my hut. Assumingly they didn't want to scrounge for materials to build another shanty, where we remained together bodies entangled for the next few weeks.

"I was fearful at first thinking it was a ruse by 'Charlie' to eavesdrop on anything my new companion and I may have said to one another. Within minutes my apprehension took second place to my over empowering needs of human touch and contact.

"His name was Gabriel a helicopter pilot running medi-vac to MASH units when he was shot down. I think we must have talked nonstop all night or until one of the guards walked by from their usual perch some 10 meters away. Gabe and I were only together for a few weeks, but it was during that time that opened my eyes to the real world around me.

I asked Gabe how he managed to survive keeping his sanity. "Tommy," he said, "My secret is nothing more than believing in the Lord's Prayer—word for word. I would repeat it to myself over and over and even over again until my heart began to feel renewed. I've been fortunate, the 'VC' hasn't used physical torture on me, and they know my job was to pickup and deliver the wounded to a field hospital. I'm just some guy who drives a whirlybird with a big red cross on its side."

I said, "Look, Gabe—I'm not what you might call a religious kind of guy, actually you might say I don't believe in God at all. I mean, if he really did exist why he hasn't shown himself to me somewhere along the way."

"But, Tommy, he has in a thousand different ways. You just didn't recognize it. Just the mere fact that you're alive proves his existence," Gabe said.

"I don't get it, Gabe, I really don't! How does my being alive prove anything?" I asked. "I've heard of your Lord's Prayer and I just can believe that this God came from the heavens up above, that's another issue, heavens from up above—the only thing up above our heads is the universe, scientists have proven that," I said.

"Tommy, are you telling me that you don't believe in God Almighty, the maker of heaven and earth or his son, Christ Jesus?" asked Gabe.

I responded by saying, "That's right, my family has always been what some people call atheists, now if someone could prove God's existence and I mean with real scientific evidence then I'm sure I would reconsider my standing. Until then, I just can't believe. I have a question for you—how can a woman have a baby who never had sex with a man? I just don't get it. It's impossible to believe—how can you? Another thing, I wished as hard as I could asking your God if he really did exist to show me a sign even to the point of taking my life so I wouldn't have to put up with another day of torment in this hell-hole…and he didn't!"

"Tommy, my naive friend, that's not the way it works. I think we need to start with praying the Lord's Prayer. What's it going to hurt anyway, what do you have to lose? So why not just humor me and let's see what might happen. Okay?" Gabs remarked with a sheepish grin on his face, he continued by saying, "Jesus, the Son of God taught his disciples to pray in this manner by bowing their heads clasping their hands saying—'Our Father which art in heaven, hallowed be thy name. Thy kingdom come, thy will be done on earth, as it is in heaven. Give us this day our daily bread, and forgive us our trespasses, as we forgive those who trespass against us. Lead us not into temptation, but deliver us from evil. For thine is the kingdom of power and glory for ever and ever. Amen.'

"That's all there is to it, Tommy. The Lord's Prayer is simple and plain but oh so meaningful. There are only three other things I want to tell you about my God, my Lord and my master. First, I know it sounds corny but God as always been my co-pilot long before I learned to fly. Second, now I'm not quoting exactly as it's written in the Bible, but it does tell us that we each must accept God on faith; the Bible even gives us a definition of what faith really is: *Faith is the substance of just knowing, the evidences not seen.* What that means to me is that I must believe that he is without it having been proven to me.

"Lastly, the Bible teaches that whenever two or more are gathered in his name he will be there also—meaning that right now, right here in this place—I think you referred to it as a hell-hole; Jesus is sitting beside us to give us strength and encouragement. That's the whole enchilada in a nutshell. It's up to you now to search your own heart and soul to find the true living Christ and accept him unconditionally for you to receive his eternal blessings. With time as you grow in the word you will learn that all that I have said is true."

We spent the next few weeks talking about the Bible, its teachings and the why and how it was written. Then one day I witnessed the VC tie Gabe down securing his stretched out arms to a pole placed behind the back of his neck forcing him into a sidecar of a motorcycle heading out of the compound. It was the first time I tried to pray on my own fearing the worst; Gabs was never seen again.

"Matthew—now I can finally answer your question about by showing up on your doorstep. I trust you more than I would trust my own brother if I had one, I need for you to confirm or simply tell me the truth about what Gabe told me…you're the only person I know who I can totally trust, I have to know the truth! Is it really as Gabs described?" Thomas asked.

I sat there mulling over what Thomas has shared with me having listened to him for hours, now he expects me to give him a simplified answer in mere minutes.

"Thomas," I said, "the first thing we need to do is ask God for guidance; asking in prayer for the power of discernment."

Thomas interrupted by saying, "Matthew that's another thing— how can I pray when I really don't understand what prayer is? I mean I may be doing it all wrong!"

"Thomas—my dear dear friend, there is no right or wrong way to pray to God. Look at it this way, when you pray to God what you are actually doing is 'talking' with him the same way you and I talk to one another. No more—no less, just talk. Start by just telling him things, asking him questions—just talk. Regardless of what you may have heard there's no orthodox holier-than-thou pious sanctimonious right or wrong way…just simple talk between the best of friends," I remarked hoping it didn't sound as if I were preaching.

"But how do I know your God hears me?" Thomas asked.

Without showing that I was beginning to feel a bit put off with what I considered ridiculous questions, the Holy Spirit gave me a gentle rap on the back of my head recalling *1 Thessalonians 5:21,* giving instruction to proof all things; I had to remind myself that Thomas was a newcomer to the family of Christ, I knew after what he had told me the hand of God touched his very soul and he was searching for explanations of God's eternal truths, and I as a steward need to be supportive of his quest.

I answered him by saying, "Let's clear something up right now, my God as you put it—is your God too, he's everyone God. As you grow in your understanding of spiritual matters you see how he is NOW, how he WAS, how he WILL ALWAYS BE," adding, "as you grow spiritually you will also come to know how he answers prayer, my prayers, your prayers everyone's prayers.

"Not to confuse matters but the Bible teaches us exactly how to pray, it also explains why our prayers made not have been heard. Thomas it's important that you read and understand 'James chapter 4' in the new testament, there you will learn that oftentimes man's prayers go unheard simply because they were not asked for in the first place and secondly they may have been asked for the wrong reasons. God knows each and everyone of us—he knows what our needs, wants and desires are even without our asking, but if we go to him in prayer we must also believe that God will grant our requests if it be his will.

"Thomas you just can't imagine how glad I am knowing that somewhere somehow the hands of the Holy Spirit has touched your soul giving you the discernment that God does in fact exist today as much now as he did when he created mankind," I said, "You will also learn the importance of God's perfect timing attach to your accepting his word on your own accord using your own free-will.

"We've known each other since we were boys playing together as best friends do, we shared everything back then from ice cream cones to spooky picture shows and even little secrets we each may have had. Do you remember how we finally agreed on the name for our neighborhood lawn mowing business, we flipped a coin but not just any old coin, it was a two-headed coin you purchased at the magic shop calling heads first so we finally settled on 'Tom & Mat's Lawn Care Extraordinaire' since you won the toss. The very next day you felt so guilty for having cheated you admitted using a rigged coin—but what you didn't know was I knew it all along, I saw the package it came in sitting on your dresser in your bedroom just the day before. If either one of us had something—it belonged to the both of us, if one of us had chores to do we did them together. We even became blood brothers by cutting our thumbs the same way we saw the 'Lone Ranger and Tonto' do; through thick and thin we shared it all except the most precious gift we could have imagined—the love of God. I had always hoped that you would one day give your life to Jesus, it only goes to show the old adage, 'That When the Student Is Ready—The Master Will Appear.'"

"Matthew—there's something else. Once we had been rescued all of the POW's from the surrounding camps within our sector were kept together as a unit and flown to a military hospital in Germany for evaluation, treatment and debriefing. During my debriefing I asked about Gabe, wondering if he had also been found knowing the Peace Keepers swept the entire geographical region where we were held. I wanted to contact him if possible needing to thank him for—well, a great many things. Although I felt like an idiot because I didn't even know his last name or what outfit he belonged to before his capture, the only info I had on Gabe was pretty vague.

"Matthew, at first it was a run of the mill inquiry, the Intel officer said he would do what he could to locate him assuring me he had found others with even less data than I had given him. I waited a few days before asking again but this time one of the medical corpsmen came to me and whispered in my ear telling me that if I persisted asking questions about Gabe, I was headed for a section 8 discharge; the release from military service reserved for mental illness. No one and I mean no one knew anything about any prisoner in any sector who was a helicopter pilot by the name of Gabe, Gabriel, Gabby or any other name closely resembling my lost acquaintance.

"The resident physician who signed-off on my medical wanted to schedule me for reconstructive surgery as soon as it could be arranged stateside telling me that the scars would be far less conspicuous. I had made-up my mind; no surgery! I wasn't about to allow someone to cut on me voluntarily even with the use of anesthetics and pain killers. Dr. Garst, M.D., was the director of the psychological science service unit at Rhein-Main Air Force Base in Germany, he told me that it wasn't at all uncommon for someone who had gone through the trauma of being held captive to fabricate or envision someone as a fellow prisoner of war easing fears of separation and isolation, a self defense survival mechanism he called it.

"Matthew as far as the military was concerned, Gabe never existed! But I know better, the time Gabe and I spent together was not a figment of my imagination, he was tangible, I felt his body as we squirmed around to lessen the intensity of spasms confined in our cramped quarters, I mean we only had a 4'X4' dugout barely five feet in height, and I assure you the conversations we had were as real as the one we are having this very moment."

I answered without hesitation, "Thomas, if you're asking me what I think—I can only tell you what I believe in my heart, at this point in time I believe based on scripture that you were in the presence of a spiritual messenger, an angel, sent to deliver a very unique message meant for you alone a message of peace and comfort. Thomas I wholeheartedly believe that angels are ever present giving help and encouragement wherever needed, sometimes we recognize the experience however more times than not we don't."

I continuing on by saying, "There are many great mysteries of which we will never be able to understand, still as a believer in the written word of Christ believing that all scripture was divinely inspired we are told that angelic beings with their sudden appearance and as well as their abrupt departure make way for prophetic reassurance as our guardian caretakers. I believe they are capable of taking on human form and when contact is made to a mortal their appearance is also as a human being, not at all like the image we envision watching television with angels coming and going on wings of flight. First of all angels don't really have wings but that's a whole different subject to deal with.

"Alright Matthew, then tell me this," asked Thomas, "if I was visited by an angel, why me, why was I so special?

"Thomas, you still don't get it do you," I said, "We are all special in the eyes of God. We each have to face difficult times and circumstances in our lives allowing us to make choices using our free-will, it is by these choices that determines if we are worthy to be called the sons of God. The Gospel of our Lord is always the same unquestionable truth, it never changes. God is always with us even when it seems as if he isn't. You ask—why were you so special, I'll tell you why! You were made in his image; you were given the mind of Christ, and after Jesus's crucifixion and resurrection you were given the comforter of the Holy Spirit the third person in the Trinity, that's why you as a child of God are special."

We said our goodbyes but this time we knelt down together giving thanks; for me a lost friend has been found, for Thomas the reassurance he so desperately searched for was over. He walked away as a true believer in the Lord Jesus Christ.

# Chapter 7: I Am but One

Each new day was as the day before, I was beginning to feel a bit over-whelmed with the world around me experiencing the notion that I had no control over my state of affairs; life is moving far too fast jumping from one issue to another like a locomotive running out of steam, without a break or reprieve. I'm feeling as if I'm being forced between here and there being pushed and pulled in so many different directions, thinking how very much like Abby's play toy Gumby must feel. How I wished I had my life back the way it was so long ago.

If only I were able to change things, to be able to take away Abby's dreaded disease and how I have dreamed—of going back in time to relive my life once again with Abigail. The thinking of Abigail has been my escape mechanism, the problem being—I really can't remember much about my life with her back then so many eon's ago.

I can recall how happy we were not having a care in the world, there were joyous times; the one that stands out above the rest was when Dr. J gave us the news that we were to be parents for a child we had hoped and prayed for, for so many years. Dr. Jenkins and Abigail held a special bond having been her family physician as a child; now by happy chance he is going to add yet another generational line to his list of patients as our child's doctor.

Thinking back I cannot remember one instance where we had a conflict or discord during the entire time we knew one another, our lives were quite giving between agreement and harmony, other than the love and comfort she gave so freely is about all I can recall. I have repressed so many memories of our lives together, things we did places we visited and for the live of me I really don't understand why I can't remember. There must be a reason—God only knows.

Now, not only do I have my concerns for my daughter, I also feel apprehensive and uneasy…admittedly I'm afraid to face the realization that LaDonna has fallen in love with me, knowing that sooner or later I'll be morally compelled to declare my feelings for her one way or another. I really haven't the strength to face another crossword puzzle of life, and don't want to think about anything other than what is absolutely necessary for daily survival.

Each day had become as the day before, and in some ways I wondered if I hadn't found comfort in my discomfort. I hadn't given much thought or attention to Aunt Cissy's theory of 'eternal perceptual visions', purposely refraining from asking Abby questions concerning her dreams. At the time I suppose I just didn't want to know. I was on over-load and stressed out to the max, as Abby would say. I wasn't ready to take-on anything else requiring thought or calibration, especially LaDonna's expressions of love.

I was holding-on the best that I knew how. I love my daughter more than life itself but if she thinks I'm going to marry LaDonna to give her solace and peace of mind, she's sadly mistaken. I believe marriage to be a sacred ordinance instituted from God as a life-long covenant creating responsibilities from both parties, which LaDonna and I have never even discussed.

Abby and I have not always agreed on everything. We have lived under the auspices that it's okay to disagree, jokingly saying that oftentimes diversity can challenge the mind. Invariably I have told Abby that our family, although just she and I, ran in a pure democratic manner and with any issue I would always ask for her opinion, I didn't always take it, but I always interested in her point of view. If for any reason I decided something contrary to her wants or desires, she would typically respond as any child would who was unable to have their own way by giving me the silent treatment or worst yet playing take-away where she would hibernate in her room until she thought I learned my lesson. I told her numerously that our family decisions were made using what knowledge we had under the umbrella of a pure benevolent dictatorship…mine. She always laughed when I made that statement, thinking it was cute I suppose, but she also knew that my decisions were not always final, having been known to change my mind, especially if she were pouting and the issue was borderline.

Abby has always known which buttons to push to get her way, thinking she has me wrapped around her little finger. But this time it won't work. If I were to marry LaDonna it must be for the right reasons. Contrary to popular belief, marriage is for all time and eternity, if LaDonna and I should ever decide to marry it will be our decision not Abby's.

One afternoon as Abby was awakening from a nap, she asked me if she and I could talk. "Dad," she said, "I love you. You're the best dad any girl could want. I know you don't want to hear this, and after everything you have done for me…well."

"What's the matter sweetheart? You know we can talk about anything," I said.

"Anything, do you really mean anything at all?" Abby asked.

"Yes dear, I really do mean anything—apparently there is something on your mind, so go ahead I'll listen," I responded.

"That's just it…I don't want you to listen—I want you to talk to me!" Abby exclaimed.

"Dad—I know you don't like talking about it, but can we talk about my mother?" Abby hesitated once again before saying, "I mean, I don't know anything about her. What was she really like? Do I look like her?" asked Abby.

I knew the day would eventually come opening my very own Pandora's Box; justifying I would cross that bridge when I came to it, making excuses to myself postponing the inescapable conversation I knew was destined to arise, thinking that there was plenty of time to tell Abby of her mother but not until I must.

I sat there speechless with a perplexed look on my face I'm sure, more surprised than anything knowing that our long awaited talk was the last thing on my mind that morning. At that precise moment I didn't know exactly what to say or how to respond. After all this time of my keeping Abigail's memory reclusive, Abby request cannot go unanswered. When Abby was a mere child of five or six years of age

I decided I would wait until she had reached the 'age of reason' somewhere around ten or twelve years old, during the interim I deliberately refrained from talking about her mother, the pain had been so deep and the scars had yet to heal. I missed my wife then, as I do now—simple words could never express the pain and loss I still feel even to this day.

When Abigail died I was devastated; I was young and had it not been for Abby, only the good Lord knows how I would have turned out. The first several weeks were the hardest to accept—that she was gone, and each time as I looked about each room within the house constant memories would drive me back into a state of depression, memories crept back into my life and I relive times and places to the point I would start crying all over again. Within a few weeks of her death Abigail's father and brother came over and moved everything we had either out of the house or into the attic out of harms way.

For my own sanity I gave away most all of the odds n' ends we had collected over the years, the sundry bric-a-brac, the knickknacks and curios, everything we shared from the linen we used to the kitchen utensils. Everything had to go; the only visible exception was the entire contents of Abby's nursery left intact just as Abigail had arranged it.

I was young and didn't know any better believing that the mental anguish would lessen accepting the fact she was gone by the removal of anything that prompted a memory of our life together. I didn't want to relive the trips we had taken, the memories associated with the art we had purchased or the furniture we sat and cuddled-up on together. The dining table where we had our meals, our LP records and 8-track tapes we listened to, the books we read together, everything.

I bought new furniture, traded in our Chevrolet for a Ford and removed every visual element of Abigail's existence except from within my heart. I couldn't stand the daily reminders of my loss by having her photographs lying around; Abigail and I had a full life together not only as spouses but as the very best of friends. Our love was so strong that we could even communicate without saying a word. More times than not we just knew what the other was thinking, feeling or about to say. We shared laughter, we shared tears…we shared all that life had to offer. Each time I made a trek to the attic, I had to mentally prepare myself for the devastation beforehand.

I remember packing some boxes of Abigail's things; I relived every moment of our life together. I couldn't stand to look at the hundreds of photograph that Abigail and I had taken throughout the years. I justified their removal by thinking that I didn't need physical photographs to remember Abigail or her love. I had all of her memories locked away in my soul, sometimes a blessing, sometimes a curse of sleepless nights.

The attic was full barely enough room to walk about. I explained to Abby that the attic was off limits because it was used for storage, not wanting her to snoop around as children might do. Not once did Abby ever question my reasoning, she knew that the Christmas decorations and the like were kept there. I explained that she might trip, stumble or fall or perhaps a heavy box stacked atop something might topple over causing injury. As a safeguard I kept the door locked with the only key on my key ring.

I seldom would go up to the attic, and when I did the pain began to fester all over again. I couldn't help myself—the mental distress was at times more than I could handle. Even with all of the grief counseling my pain was still so overwhelming, so consuming my every moment, so deafening I could hear my heart beat. I tried sharing in support groups with people who have undergone a similar experience thinking it might be comforting, it wasn't. It wasn't until I allowed Christ to share in my grief that I was able to find acceptance.

The Bible tells us there is a time to weep; as sure as night turns to day, my mind began recalling scriptures I had read bringing a new light of understanding granting permission for me to feel my loss.

Abraham wept and mourned the death of his wife Sarah, even our savior Jesus Christ wept at the graveside of his friend Lazarus. With great soul-searching I finally realized that what I was feeling was a loss for what was to come; following the current day, the next day and the day after that and so on, I no longer knew what to expect as I did when Abigail was alive. As always it was she and I as one.

Then one day while asking God's forgiveness for my selfish behavior I realized the feelings I experienced in the attic wasn't sorrow at all, but was actually outrage—I was maddened because she left me.

As an educator whenever my students suffered disagreement I made them sit-down and rethink why they became angry in the first place hoping to find resolution by understanding the core of their anger. Throughout Christian writings theologians have listed seven deadly sins, one of them being belligerence or anger, an act that is regarded by a transgression of God's will. It was only after great prayer and self-examination that I reached a level of acceptance based upon searching my heart for the truth. The truth was—Abigail didn't leave me, she died; as a Christian believing that death is part of God's eternal plan I fell to my knees in prayer asking God to forgive me for my failure to accept his will.

Once my heart and mind became as one, God removed the veil that I had placed upon my own eyes having found peace from within myself, from that point on I was able to return to the attic and could actually reminisce with Abigail in a spiritual sense.

Naturally there were special times throughout the years that I would go to retrieve an item or two such as holiday decorations, then again, there were also times I would go just to feel close to Abigail. I would sit on an antique settee; the same one she kept at the foot of our bed, all the while clutching our wedding photo. I missed her so, I accepted she was gone but somehow the physical remains of our life together gave me strength to carry on for Abby. I would oftentimes just sit and pray, and talk aloud as if she were present. I would talk about our daughter and how she was growing; tell her how she was doing in school, and how the little Smith boy had such a crush on her in the first grade. I never had any secrets from Abigail; the attic had become our place…, my sanctuary. Oh, I knew that Abigail didn't really hear me, or did she I wondered. Somehow I just felt better thinking that she was listening; I always seemed to have a clearer outlook and felt warmth after one of our talks.

The Bible says that 'the dead know not at all', and then again another verse tells us that upon out death 'the spirit returns from where it came', for me personally I choose to believe that her spirit has ears to hear my plight.

The time has finally come that I have dreaded so. I knew that someday I would have to face the issues with Abby concerning her mother. I never really wanted to, several times I started to, but each time I backed out because of fear. I couldn't find any rational reason how her knowing could be of any benefit, thinking Abby might blame herself for her mother's death. There was no one to blame, life and death are both in the hands of God. I prayed that Abby would understand and forgive me, knowing why I did what I did, never intending to deceive her of her birth right of knowing her mother.

I sat there and held Abby's hand as I spoke, really talking as never before. I exposed my most inner thoughts explaining how very deep the love was that her mother and I shared. I told her how Abigail and I believed that our whole relationship was created at the beginning of time. Once I started sharing with Abby the fears that I had held for so many years just seem to vanish, I knew that my Guardian Angel was present directing my words.

Abby didn't say a word, she just listened.

I continued by relaying event after event giving reference to the life that her mother and I shared together. We talked the better part of the afternoon late into the evening, finally when her dinner tray arrived she gave way to continue on later, reluctantly.

Abby was captivated, learning not only of her mother but her grandparents as well. All of her life the only thing that I deliberately wanted to keep from her was the consequence of her mother's death. I never intended to keep her family genealogy a secret. As sick as she was, she insisted on wanting to know more.

Having eaten her dinner she was anxious to know more about her mother. I cleaned off the adjustable roll-a-way hospital table placing in the center of the table a leather bound keepsake photo album much too heavy for her to hold, having retrieved it from the attic just weeks beforehand where it had sat undisturbed all these years. Inside the album were old photographs, mementoes and souvenirs that Abigail had painstakingly placed between its now yellowing pages. I said most everything I could think of, telling her to go through the album herself, saying that later we could continue-on because I was becoming fatigued and fading-out quickly.

Knowing my daughter as I did, I purposely leaned back in my recliner, closed my eyes and pretended to drift off in a nap. I knew that Abby was wired with excitement and LaDonna's presence would at least give me a reprieve to gather my thoughts. I also thought that it would be a good way to see how LaDonna would react to the photo album. Feigning sleep, I eavesdropped to the conversation that Abby was having with LaDonna.

"Mom, is Dad really asleep?" Abby asked LaDonna.

LaDonna must have nodded her head because I didn't hear any response. Abby continued by saying, "Can you believe it? Dad was actually telling me about my real mother. Did you know that one time my mother threw a chocolate cream pie in my father's face? It was some sort of charity church function. You know, Dad—he's always so prim and proper, can you imagine chocolate pie all over his face? I bet it was funny. He also told me how…oh LaDonna, I'm sorry. I guess maybe I shouldn't talk about her…you know, with you I mean. I don't want you to think that…but, you're the closest thing to a mother I have ever known, and I would love you even if I wasn't, you know dying. You do love Dad, right? I mean that kinda makes us like a real family then—right."

"That's okay sweetheart, everything's okay. Don't worry about it, it doesn't bother me to talk to you about your birth mother," answered LaDonna. "It's only natural to want to talk about your mother, especially since your dad has kept her such a secret."

"It's really okay with you?" Abby questioned.

"Yes, darling, it really is," LaDonna said. "I'm not trying to take her place, I never could. Abby, I love you even though I'm not your natural mother—remember what I told you, love doesn't come with a set of instructions—it just is. I'm glad you want to share the memories of your birth mother with me."

"But what about Dad?" Abby asked.

"What about your dad?" LaDonna questioned.

"You know…you loving my dad, I mean," Abby said.

The room became silent, as if the two of them had left. Within a few seconds I felt LaDonna placing a covering over my lap and legs, believing it to have been the hand made afghan that LaDonna knitted for Abby several months ago. The smell of LaDonna's perfume embedded within the yarn gave it a special scent of warmth. Within moments I overheard LaDonna and Abby carry on their conversation.

"Abby," LaDonna said. "I wanted to make sure your father was really asleep. Look just between us girls, we still have to stick together. Your father is the most caring man I have ever known. He's kind, he's considerate, and he's good looking too. He's everything any woman could ever want in a man. He has principles and values, he believes in God, he has a good job and yes, I do love him. But he doesn't know it, and you can't tell him! Now promise me—you won't say a word. He has more on his shoulders now than he deserves to carry; his only concern right now should be you. For the time being we need to keep this conversation hush-hush, your dad knows I like him, but he hasn't a clue that I have fallen in love with him. It's extremely important that this remain our little secret for a little while longer."

"But LaDonna, you need to tell him. I want you to tell him. I know my dad, and he needs to know just how you feel. Look, Dad is always telling me that God has perfect timing. Does it matter how you and Dad met? Does it really matter? Remember what you told me, love doesn't come with a set of instructions—it just is. Neither one of you should be thinking of me, in the long term. You both need to think about yourselves for a change. Besides, after I'm gone, you and Dad would be perfect for each other. You both love each other, and I know my dad loves you, too, I just know he does. You're perfect together. Am I the only one who can see it? You're both so afraid and I don't understand why," said Abby.

"Abby, your father and I aren't afraid of anything," said LaDonna. "Sometimes as adults we tend to be, well, a bit more cautious and discreet with our feelings. Think back when you first realized that Bobby had a crush on you. How did it make you feel knowing he liked you? Did it make you happy or sad knowing that he wanted to spend time with you, walk you home from school and carry your books? Didn't you tell me you felt confused? Can't you remember telling me that you were more concerned about what your father might say than what you were feeling or thinking about Bobby? What about the time Bobby kissed you on the cheek at the water fountain and ran away only to come back later wanting to hold your hand during recess? How many times did he offer you something from the lunch sack that his mother had packed for him? It may have been only a candy bar, or a cookie or a piece of fruit, but he wanted to share something, anything just as long as he could be near you.

"What I am trying to say is that relationships for adults are the same way too. Sometimes we want to share something with another, and sometimes we don't have anything to share except pieces of ourselves. Honey, I know you liked Bobby and it was obvious that he liked you. But the two of you had to like each other at the same time. The same is true for your father and I. Regardless of how I may feel, unless the time is just right and your father has the same kind of feelings as I do, we will have to remain just friends. Until then, we can only share what is ours to give. Your dad right now is running on empty and has nothing else to give or share with me or anyone.

"Abby your dad's entire being right now is unselfishly wrapped around you and your world. I love your father as much as any woman could, enough so, not wanting to place any more pressures or restrains on him or upon his time. Right now your father has tunnel vision and each day is a struggle in itself. I'm not worried about what the future may hold, and you shouldn't either. Abby, can you understand what I am saying? It's alright sometimes to love from a distance. Sweetheart, I'm so grateful for having been included in both of your lives this past year, I've seen more love between you and your father in this very room then most people experience in a lifetime. Besides, tell me where is it written that I must receive love in order to give love. Now promise me, you won't say anything."

"I promise," said Abby. "But it won't be easy keeping such a big secret."

I didn't know how much longer I could lie there in silence. Both Abby and LaDonna had said things that had touched my very soul. I wanted to get-up from that chair and hug them both. I wanted to, but couldn't. If I had, I might have been placed in a position to acknowledge feelings that I have suppressed for LaDonna. The two of them were so very right, but for different reasons.

I sat there a bit longer than reached out and stretched as if arising from a deep sleep.

"I'm sorry ladies; I didn't mean to fall asleep. How long was I out? Did I miss anything?" I asked.

"You only napped for a little while Dad and what could you have possibly missed anyway ask yourself. Dad, LaDonna is making me eat my green beans again. Gosh, I mean—I hate green beans," Abby replied in what she thought was a cute and witty manner saying, "I know I'm suppose to eat all my vegetables because I need the vitamins and minerals to help keep my strength up, right."

"Darling, you know what Dr. J said that you needed to eat your weight in green beans, spinach and carrots," said LaDonna. "Isn't it better than taking those vitamin injections?"

"Yea, yea, it's better, but they still taste bad." Abby uttered.

"LaDonna, if it's okay with you I think I'll go down to the cafeteria and eat some green beans myself," I said.

LaDonna looked up smiled saying, "Sure Matthew, don't worry about us, besides it just gives us a little more time for some girl talk. Besides it's time for Abby to get up out of her bed so I can change her sheets—Abby can sit in your recliner while you're gone. Now take your time and give us about half an hour or so. By the way, I just happen to have a movie I rented here in my bag and thought that the three of us might watch it later on. Are you up for a movie?" "Sounds good to me," I said. "How about you Abby, okay with you?"

Abby just smiled and gave LaDonna a wink. She didn't think I understood, but I did. Her little non-verbal communication speaks volumes much louder than words.

As I started to walk out the door, the door swung open and entered Aunt Cissy. "Hello everybody," she said, "How's every little thing this fine evening?

"Fine, Aunt Cissy." Abby answered.

"Can I lean over and give my best girl a kiss?" asked Aunt Cissy.

"Sure thing, Auntie," said Abby.

Aunt Cissy leaned over and gently held Abby as she gave her kiss on her cheek. "My dear," she said, "you just get prettier each and every day. It's no wonder why your father never wants to leave your side. He's afraid that some young doctor may steal you away from him."

Abby tried to laugh, but she was becoming weary, she hadn't had her nap as of yet and sometimes even smiling could be draining. Abby's timeline of hours in any given day are subjective to how she may be feeling from one moment to the next.

"Matthew, last night I made some chocolate chip cookies and I sure could use your opinion. If you have a minute stop by and taste one for me." Aunt Cissy said. "LaDonna, by the way, I have a pair of tickets for the planetarium if you could talk Matthew into taking you. If you like I could sit with Abby; we could have one of our sessions allowing you and Matthew a little break from these four walls. Just let me know, say, when Matthew comes down to my office for a cookie why don't you tag-along," she said.

LaDonna leaned over and whispered in Abby's ear saying, "I liked the way that sounded when Aunt Cissy said, 'You and Matthew', what do you think? Do you think he even has a clue?"

I could see the sly guileful looks upon their faces and hear an ever so faint girlish giggle between them.

"Aunt Cissy, I was just leaving to grab a bite of lunch. Would you care to join me?" I asked.

"No thank you Matthew. I have a few things to do. Don't forget, I have cookies for you in my office. I'll see you in what, about an hour or so. Good...I better go for now. See everybody later. Bye," remarked Aunt Cissy.

I opened the door as Aunt Cissy exited; standing in the doorway I turned around and asked LaDonna if she wanted me to bring her something back from the cafeteria. She shook her head no, but then remarked that she and I could share a cookie with Aunt Cissy after I returned.

Sitting in the dining room I began to play with my food pushing my meal around the plate, my mind kept going back to the conversation I overheard between Abby and LaDonna. God knows that I love them both, but I wonder why then do I feel such a dilemma where LaDonna is concerned, definitely a lack of clear and orderly thought.

I remember Abigail telling me before we married that whenever two hearts truly touch, they would never again be far apart.

LaDonna has been a great help with Abby, she is a fantastic woman, tender and affectionate and most of all giving. I'm sure if things were quite different I would have no trouble opening up my heart to LaDonna, but it's been so long since I allowed myself the freedom to feel the love of a good woman.

Abby is right about one thing…I am afraid, afraid that I might never be able to love LaDonna with the same love that I had for Abigail.

I am but one man attempting to do my best, sometimes it seems as though my best isn't good enough. The second we are born the clock starts ticking away and it is only by our choices that we are recognized for our beliefs and values.

I am but one who is father, I am but one who has accepted Christ Jesus as his personal savior, I am but one man who may or may not be prepared for what is yet to come.

In the final analysis when we each stand before the judgment seat of Christ will we not all feel—I am but one.

# Chapter 8: The Cornerstone of Four

As a father I question if I have prepared my child sufficiently to meet Jesus Christ without fear of fault, even more so knowing that my daughter is definitely without question with absolute resolve dying sometime in the very near future.

One day last week the hospital chaplain came by to see me, not Abby but me, to see if I was in need of comfort or support during my time of trial as he put it, telling me quote, "You should be grateful your daughter has not reached the age of accountability," continuing on to say, "rest assured God has special dispensation for children and your daughter is ascertained a place God's heavenly kingdom. I couldn't believe what I had heard as if she were exempt from sin simply because of her age. He's teaching what he believes to be true but if he researched a little deeper he would know that statement such as his are totally false and without merit. I don't know what Protestant denomination he was or do I care, but had he really understood his Bible he would know that the phrase 'age of accountability' isn't in the Bible—not even once. In fact, the concept itself is really not discussed in the Holy Scripture anywhere.

Throughout the entire text of the Old and New Testament biblical scholars have theorized making conjecture by using obscure examples of what God may have been thinking. I ask you—'Who knows the mind of God'?

Almost all scripture in the Bible concerning the teaching of children are addressed to their male parent, the fathers; Proverbs 4:1-2 is an example: *'Listen, my sons, to a father's instruction; pay attention and gain understanding. I give you sound learning, so do not forsake my teaching.'* God has spiritually prepared men to fulfill this role, giving guidance by way of the holy scriptures compelling fathers to talk to their children not only about his commandments but essential chaste virtues in living a just lifestyle, as referenced by reading 'Deuteronomy 6:7' where the Bible tells us to talk to our children at all times about all things.

As a father if I fail to read and learn from God's inspired writings, how then can I teach my daughter giving eternal guidance as God has commanded me to do?

Abby and I have our prayer time each day, separately and collectively having set aside specific times each week for Bible study, generally Sunday late afternoons before dinner and at least one hour during the week whenever we can arrange the time. Finding time to study the word of God intently is not as easy as you might think, and must be done without the added burden of feeling tired or stressed out from normal day to day endeavors.

My obligation outside the classroom has always been a balancing-act between grading papers, parent conferences, staff meetings and Abby's extracurricular activities. Between her piano lessons, dance classes, Girl Scouts and her young women's group meetings at church only made it more interesting when trying to manipulate our timeline to set aside yet one more scheduled event of Bible study. Trying to keep focused on learning the word of God can be difficult. In order to achieve the most of what little time we have budgeted.

I would first select chosen passages from the Holy Scriptures with regards to a specified trait or characteristic which I felt Abby and I needed to read and study together, having read the selected topic myself beforehand to gain understand myself.

When Abby came in from school one day she relayed an incident in her classroom of a classmate not only stealing, an item of insignificant value, but lied and tried to conceal his act. It was opportunities such as this that directed me to specific areas of Bible study relevant to Abby's religious instruction.

"Abby," I would say, "Remember my child, Satan is the father of all lies. Can you think about the very first lie we find in the Bible?

Think about it—okay, what about the statement the snake made to Eve in the garden?" Abby sat there with a look on her face as if were to say 'oh yeah', I continued by saying, "By reading Exodus 20:16 we learn as Christians we should always tell the truth. Sweetheart, I'm paraphrasing, but if I were to summarize what it says it would be 'not to lie to anyone about anything.' Sweetheart, how many commandants do you think that little boy broke when he first took something that wasn't his and then tried to cover it up by lying about it, how many? Think about the 8$^{th}$, 9$^{th}$ and 10$^{th}$ Commandments—do you think they might be applicable here?

Abby, one of my favorite Bible passages is Proverbs 6, where the Lord is telling us certain things about how we should live our life. Among all the examples there, He said he hated *a lying tongue*; I don't think I can put it any simpler.

During various other Bible sessions Abby and I discussed the importance of living in a day-to-day relationship with the Lord God in "Deuteronomy 6:4-9", "Jeremiah 9:24", and "Philippians 3:8-10", to know the joy of obedience and the value of building personal character found in "Genesis 18:19", "Philippians 2:19-22", and learning the necessary life skills for getting along in the world as directed by "Proverbs 22:29", these are just a few examples, and there are countless others.

I do believe a child's spiritual accountability will be held to a different standard than that of an adult who has lived a full life, each child is a unique individual in the eyes of God, and I also believe God does not hold those accountable who are incapable of understanding the transgression of his will. With accountability comes enormous responsibility; accountability requires the capability of conscious choices when making decisions using free-will along with the understanding of the consequences that may follow to any given act, as we learn by reading "Daniel 12: 10", "Many will be purified, made spotless and refined, but the wicked will continue to be wicked. None of the wicked will understand, but those who are wise will understand."

Having not had to swim the turbulent waters of Abby's teenage years some issues have never come into play, like sexual experimentation or promiscuousness. Abby knows and understands the sexuality of human desire is not unlike any other physical driving force that mankind must face on a day to day basis. She knows that abstinence before marriage was God's plan from the beginning of time, that God created sex to be a blessing of the union between a husband and wife, but he clearly and absolutely disapproves of all other sexual activity, including premarital sex—"Marriage is honorable among all, and the bed undefiled; but fornicators and adulterers God will judge." Hebrew 13:4.

Abby and I have discussed the role of human sexuality since the first time she came to me with a question. Parent's and children have a unique special bond created at birth with their roles well defined by the scriptures, and who better than to educate and instruct children than the parents. How can one's sexuality, or sex itself be taught to a child by a complete stranger? Even as an educator I believe sexual information and training belongs in the home where It should be taught between people who love and hold that special bond; showing that sex is a very personal private matter allowing the children the opportunity to ask questions freely and not feel intimidated because their peer's might find it amusing if forced to acquire the same knowledge in the classroom or worst yet on the streets from older children.

There is a time in the development of a child's life that they may not know to choose good and refuse evil, this I believe corresponds to the maturity level found in the child. There is however no excuse for a child not having learned the basic principles and tenets of God's eternal plan for salvation.

Abby has reached her age of reason and is quite the little scholar for barely being twelve years of age. She knows and believes with certainty that God is the great "I AM"; has a good understanding of the four cardinal virtues of life which can be difficult concepts for some adults I have known.

I explained to Abby the "four cardinal virtues" by simplifying the phrase itself. *Four* as a numeral representation, *cardinal* explaining the root word comes from the Latin translation "cardo or cardin" literal translation to mean *hang/hinge* and *virtues* is nothing more than doing what is right and avoiding what is wrong, the opposite of virtue being a "vice" which is a transgression of moral character.

I explained that of the four cardinal virtues, "Prudence" meant developing wisdom, "Temperance" was learning self-control with moderation, "Fortitude" was developing courage to see something through and "Justice" meant to display righteousness in all that we do.

I explained that all other virtues in life must stem from these four, hence "hinged" or "stemmed from" as a foundation or building blocks for other virtues to rest upon; without these four virtues as a foundation all other virtues in life are quite impossible to achieve. If a person lacks fortitude he will not have the courage to overcome the difficulties practicing any other virtue. If he is not prudent he will lack the wisdom necessary to understand what he is doing, if he lacks temperance he will not be able to control his own physical drives and appetites, and lastly **justice** to be fair in all of our dealings free from discrimination or dishonesty.

In order for Abby to fully appreciate the different virtues I devised a little systematic word game she and I would play every so often. We might be driving down the street together or standing outside in the backyard grilling steaks on the BBQ pit, she and I would take turns—whoever thought about playing the game was allowed to go first which always seemed to have a bit of advantage. One of us would begin by going through the letters of the alphabet submitting a virtue beginning with that given letter "A", "B", and "C" and so on; over time, we were able to compile quite a list of desirable traits. There were only two rules of the game; rule one, we could start anywhere in the alphabet but the second player was required to follow placement to whatever the given letter started with. Rule two stipulated that we give a brief definition of each virtue. One of us may start out by saying, "Altruism is the practice of placing others before oneself." Abby would then think a moment and take her turn, "Beautiful in spirit." We continued on as time permitted always playing our little game while in the pursuit of doing something else, folding laundry, doing the dishes, etc. etc. etc. Honesty is the human quality of communicating and acting truthful, Integrity shows someones character to be beyond reproach, Mercy related to concepts of justice and morality in behavior between people, Nurture is defined as the process of caring for and teaching a child as the child grows, Understanding is a process whereby one is able to think and use concepts to deal adequately with any given subject, Wisdom is the ability to make correct judgments and decisions and Zealousness is marked by active interest and enthusiasm. The only letter of the alphabet we were not able to find a true virtue without using the word as "Quality" this or that, was the letter "Q."

She is far beyond understanding the divergences merely between right and wrong; she has a solid grasp of Christianity's theological virtues of faith, hope and charity which comes from the New Testament 1 Corinthians 13:13, which she memorized in the first grade.

As I stared at my plate of half-eaten food I prayed silently asking God to give me guidance where I may have failed in Abby's spiritual education. Accountability before God regardless of age is an individual matter, one which varies dramatically with each person, and which ultimately is known only to God.

I looked at my watch and realized that I had wasted enough time lingering over my tasteless meal. I haven't had much of an appetite since Abby first became ill; then again hospital food has never had the reputation of being fine cuisine. From the onset I have eaten or shall I say attempted to eat 312 meals down here in the cafeteria, I know that because one day out of sheer boredom I calculated the number of days and the average meals I could should have eaten and can up with the number 312.

The girls were probably waiting impatiently for me upstairs. LaDonna and I are to go to Aunt Cissy's office for some of her celebrated chocolate chip cookies, I must admit they're great, but then, anything homemade is greatly appreciated to my way of thinking; I wonder what she really has on her mind.

Just as I was about to enter the elevator the hospital PBX operator paged me, "Mr. Matthew Anderson, please call extension 359. Extension 359, please."

Extension 359—that's Abby's room extension I thought to myself, she probably wants to know why I have taken so long. I had one foot in the elevator deciding that instead of turning around trying to locate a telephone, it would be faster just to get on the elevator and go to Abby's room. The page in itself didn't concern me; several of the doctor's have summoned me in the past when I wasn't in Abby's room. It wasn't the first time, so I gave it little concern.

As the elevator doors opened on Abby's floor, LaDonna was frantically standing there waiting for me, sobbing and shrieking out of control. "Matthew, it's Abby…she went into sudden cardiac arrest just a few minutes ago," she said.

I stood there in shock. "Is she gone?" I asked as my body began to quiver.

"No, thank God," she responded. "Doctor Questa and his team are working on her right now. If she can be stabilized, she'll most likely be transported to ICU's cardiac care center."

I turned around and started to open up the door to Abby's room only to be met by Dr. Questa, a fifth-year resident from the cardiac care center; at that exact moment LaDonna pulled herself close to my chest before he could speak.

"Mr. Anderson, to come straight to the point—she's barely alive, we have her as stable as we can, in a few moments my team will transfer her to our care center where we can monitor her vitals, I need to ask—have you signed a DNR?"

LaDonna responded without thinking, saying, "We have one on file for oncology—we need to amend it to include all medical procedures."

"Matthew, I'm sorry," LaDonna said. "When she stopped breathing I didn't have the opportunity to have you paged until help arrived. Aunt Cissy was the first one here just seconds before Dr. Questa; she pushed me out of the room, saying I was much too close to Abby to be objective or to be of any help."

"Hold me, Matthew. Hold me close," LaDonna exclaimed.

LaDonna and I stood there holding each other in a tender embrace standing outside Abby's room, both of us crying as only a grieving parent could understand. We shared feelings of despair, of hopelessness and melancholy without speaking a word. We each knew what the other was feeling and tried to give one another comfort, knowing this could well be the end.

For well over an hour Dr. Questa's cardiac care crisis team worked on Abby before she would be moved. It was the first time LaDonna and I prayed together for our darling Abby. Instantly, without thought, I knew Abby was right, I did have feelings for LaDonna, intimate feelings I no longer wished to hide—at last I realized that LaDonna and I were in this together. By the grace of God and his multitude of angels, we both would be there for Abby until the very end.

When the door finally opened to Abby's room, LaDonna and I jumped to our feet to find Aunt Cissy who was came to come out. She walked over to both LaDonna and I, gave us a three-way hug, positioning herself between us. She grabbed us both by our elbows, turning us around and proceeded to lead us down the opposite end of the hall as the team made its way to the cardiac care ICU with Abby. As I looked over my shoulder, Aunt Cissy tried to block my view; however, I could see them rolling Abby down the hall hurriedly.

I could see that the gurney was covered with various pieces of life support equipment and apparatus, intravenous bags hung from each corner of the gurney with lines running to various parts of her body. I could see tubes coming out of her nose and mouth. I could see all of this; but I couldn't see her face.

"Matthew, don't be an alarmist. LaDonna will explain to you the necessity of what is now being done," said Aunt Cissy. "The doctors will be out to see both of you as soon as they have her set up in the ICU. LaDonna, get hold of yourself and take Matthew to the ICU waiting room. It shouldn't be very long before we have an updated prognosis on her condition. Now go!"

LaDonna was as visibly sickened as I was. I had no doubts that her love for my daughter was as great as mine. For the better part of just a little less than two years, she had been by Abby's side almost as much as I have. LaDonna could not have loved her anymore if she were her biological mother.

We sat and waited together holding hands. Strange, but prior to today, we never showed any outward display of affection to one another, not even a friendly kiss. From the very beginning she and Abby shared endearments, but never she and I. Surprisingly LaDonna and I were both in a state of panic and disbelief over Abby's condition, we each had a great deal of time to prepare ourselves for the inevitable, but somehow didn't accept that 'one day'—could be today. Neither one of us wanted to accept that the unpleasant and disastrous day of reckoning was finally here, but we both agreed that her life was in the hands of God.

LaDonna knew the nursing staff in the ICU, and they kept us abreast while the doctor's did what they felt best in stabilizing Abby's life.

"LaDonna, can I be honest with you, without your thinking I'm some sort of a monster? I mean, a few minutes ago I started to plead with God to take her. I didn't, but I did think about it. Does that make me weak, or seem like a terrible father?" I said.

"No Matthew," LaDonna replied. "It doesn't make you a terrible father. On the contrary, it only makes you human. It's only natural to want God to ease suffering, especially for a loved one, a child. God understands our hearts and our minds. It's no sin to think about something that may be contrary to God's will, it's only when we act upon our thoughts that oppose his will, when it becomes a sin. Remember God's promised that he would never place a burden on our shoulders greater than we can handle. I think you have done a marvelous job raising Abby, especially since she became ill. I've never seen any father sacrifice for a child as you have. Abby is so blessed to have you for a father; for heaven's sake, give yourself some credit."

LaDonna and I sat impatiently for approximately thirty minutes and still no word from the doctor's. We purposely positioned ourselves just outside those automated double doors, thinking that as they opened we might just get a glimpse of what was going on inside. The longer it seemed to take, the more my mind talk ran away with my emotions.

It seemed like a lifetime but finally Dr's. Questa and Jenkins emerged from behind those double doors that held the fate of my darling daughter. Before he could speak LaDonna reached out and grabbed my hand, looked into my eyes and said "Matthew, we will come through this, I know it's going to be all right. I just know it is."

Dr. Jenkins had a solemn look on his face one that I could only describe as being somber, it was not a look that I cared for, nor was it a look that I felt easy with, Dr. Questa stood silently by his side.

"Matthew, LaDonna," Dr. J said. "There are many great joys in the field of medicine. That's the reason I became a doctor in the first place some sixty years ago. Still, it's never seems to get any easier when it necessitate being the bearer of bad news. Dr. Questa asked that I speak with you knowing we have had numerous discussions preparing for what was to come. As you know—my attachment to Abby is much more than just a doctor patient relationship. I love that little girl just as I loved her mother when she was that age. It's unpleasant to have to say this, but her time has come and there is absolutely little else we can do, and I might add…should do. Matthew, remember the discussion we had concerning the right to life? I'm sorry Matthew, but you must now decide that if and when she should ever have another attack, do we attempt to resuscitate or not? As her father the decision lies with you, my recommendation is to allow her to peacefully go without any added efforts regardless of medical causation or inducement. But the decision must be yours alone."

"Mark, you know how I feel. I don't want her body living by artificial and synthetic means, I believe it's unnatural. That's the reason I agreed to hospice care foregoing all medical intervention. I don't believe God intended man to prolong live by using gadgets and gizmos, tubes, and wires. No! My feelings haven't changed. When she becomes unable to breath on her own then it's time, time for Abby to drift off in sleep relinquishing her spirit to return from where it came. I know she's ready. No life support system, not now, not ever." Matthew exclaimed with tear laded eyes. "Please Mark allow her to die with dignity."

Dr. Questa handed me the DNR forms and I signed them without any hesitancy.

"Matthew, go ahead and sign the papers—it's for the best," LaDonna said. "Doctors, can we have a few minutes alone, please?"

"LaDonna," Matthew said, "when it happens, I may not be as strong as you think I am. In fact, I know I'm not. I'm going to need you to lean on, I don't have the answers and frankly I don't think mankind as the ability to fully understand God will. Were only given glimpses of discernment, Jesus himself said there would be many great mysteries of life, and I think this just happens to be one of them.

"I've questioned over and over…who am I to play God? But during the interim when it's all said and done, I have, I mean…I have chosen to place the mantle of God upon my shoulders determining life or death for my daughter by telling the doctor's not to revive or resuscitate her. A day didn't go by down in the oncology ward and then her transfer to the hospice that I fail to question myself; is this the right decision, how can I know? LaDonna, what gives me the right to be able to make such a decision? Naturally I don't want to see her suffer but then again, who am I to judge? God gave us the breath of life; now you tell me, do I…does anyone have the right to extend or extinguish that breath beyond what he may have intended? How can I even question what his intentions may be? How can anyone?"

"Peter, Mark, can we see her now?" Matthew asked.

"Yes, but there's one last thing," he said. "Abby—has not regained consciousness, she's comatose—she could wake-up at any moment or quite possibly never. She is however breathing on her own, her heart never stopped beating and I can only assume at this point that her arrest was the result of irregular heart rhythm what we call arrhythmia which causes the heart to suddenly stop beating in a normal manner. In Abby's case it's called bradycardia an extreme slowing of the heart.

"Now let's not be fooled—she is definitely at risk for another arrest, it's a wonder her heart has make it this far considering everything the cancer has put her body through. I just can't fully explain what actually happened, her heart rate miraculously returned to what I would consider normal for her medical condition, without our having to shock her. I'm sorry, but I can't tell you anymore than what I have."

LaDonna and I walked into the ICU followed by Mark and Peter. It's sad to say, but the room by itself permeated with the smell of death. The sight of Abby lying there, lifeless, attached to all of the amenities that modern medicine had to offer was almost more than I could handle, reminding me of the condition she was in not that long ago. Her room in the hospice at least offered some ray of dignity. Here in the ICU, one could calculate the degree of life and death, by mere numbers.

Without rehearsal LaDonna and I went to opposite sides of Abby's bed, my heart ached recalling that merely two hours ago she was awake and teasing me about green beans. The notion if I had only stayed with her instead of going down to the cafeteria, I could have been with her when she needed me the most—kept running through my mind. LaDonna and I formed a prayer circle, the three of us holding hands as I prayed for my child's life. In the name of Jesus Christ I prayed for compassion, for understanding and for strength.

LaDonna and I stood by her bedside speaking only with our eyes dealing with the grief and uncertain torment of Abby's condition in our own separate ways, me as her father, LaDonna not only as a nurse but now as her mother.

I had an overwhelming feeling that Abby would never leave the ICU, saying a silent prayer to my Father in Heaven asking for his blessing on my daughter's soul.

"LaDonna," I said. "Would you please do me a favor? Could you find Aunt Cissy and give me a few minutes alone with Abby?"

After LaDonna left I stood there motionless as if time had stopped; my train of thought envisioned our lives together as if being shown on a movie projector frame by frame. As I stood there holding her tiny withered hands thinking of things both large and small, the insignificant and monumental moments we shared together as parent and child recalling every tear she had shed, both the happy and the sad. I thought back to her first day in school, her first crush on a boy and her first home cooked meal she prepared for me all by herself without my help. I also thought how unfortunate life would be for those, who would never know the love and tenderness of this darling little girl. I found myself recalling nostalgic sentimental emotional feelings, which only I as her father could fully appreciate. I remembered the very last time she told me she loved me, the last time I told her no when in fact I wanted to say yes over some silly little thing she wanted not wanting to spoil her anymore than she already was.

She never asked for much or anything that I would have considered elaborate or foolish. For a child of twelve she is quite sensible using sound judgment and common sense in practical matters.

I thought back to our last Bible study in great detail that Abby and I had together before she became ill; we were reading in the New Testament where Paul the Apostle wrote a letter to Timothy who was in Ephesus, I explained to Abby that Ephesus was a thriving ancient city located in southwestern Asia in what is known today as western Turkey. Paul was giving instruction to what should be taught in the church telling Timothy that he should take special care to avoid the stories, legends and fables from the old teachings saying that in the final analysis the end result of all of God's commandants was nothing less than the love; love of God, love of our fellow man and love for the church. Paul was telling Timothy that *Charity* was showing love for his fellowman in all things with a *Pure Heart* by living a life without having malice, envy or pride against anyone based upon *Faith Unfeigned*, living a life without worldly pretense or fear of what other's may think, having a *Good Conscience*, which is living a life in a righteous manner, the cornerstone of four of the seven preeminent virtues ennobling faith for the church.

I also made reference to Matthew 22: 37 where Jesus said, "Thou shall love the Lord thy God with all thy heart, and with all thy soul, and with all thy might. This is the first and great commandment. And a second command is like unto it, thou shall love thy neighbor as thyself. On these two commandments hang all the laws given to the prophets."

I explained to Abby that the key word in the verse was the word 'hang' referring to something else that has a correlation as a foundation to build upon.

"Ya know, Dad," Abby commented, "the way I see it is, if a person really loves and believes in God they wouldn't be worshiping images like the golden calf the Hebrew people did. I bet-ya it really blew Moses's mind when he came off Mount Sinai with the stone tablets God gave him engraved with the ten commandants and saw what his brother Aaron did. Dad, answer me this, the Bible tells us that no man has ever seen the face of God and as believers we accept that 'God is' on faith—right, well then how can anybody worship an object and that's all it is, an object—something made by the hands of man. God tells us we look like him, I mean, we were created in his image, and…what I don't get—is why some people made graven images of animals to worship. I mean what does the likeness of an animal have to do with the image of God anyway? Another thing, too, how could anyone in their right mind dare to blaspheme God. You have always told me that words are very powerful—and to blaspheme the Holy Spirit is unforgivable; you told me that the definition of blasphemy is to deny the Holy Spirit's witness to Jesus, but I still don't get it."

"Okay, darling, let me explain it this way," I said. "In the beginning, God told Adam and Eve everything they needed to know to live peacefully in the garden for all eternity, and didn't always give his reasons why they were what they were. We may not always know or understand why something is wrong or inappropriate; but just the knowing that God considers it wrong makes each of us accountable for the act as if we understood the reasons behind his thinking. The bottom line is really simple, *the only sin God can't forgive is the sin of rejecting Christ*—that's what the scripture's meant by indicating blasphemy against the Holy Ghost is a eternal sin. Understand now?"

I continued on by saying, "But let's look at something else a little closer; if we truly love our neighbor is it possible to rob or steal from them, or deliberately hurt or murder them?"

Abby just sat there shaking her head and then said, "Dad, I remember you telling me that there was a translation problem with the ten commandants that the original Hebrew text used the word 'murder' not 'kill' like we see in our Bibles. Why do our Bibles say kill instead of the way it was suppose to be written?"

"Abby," I said, "we have to remember that some words used in the Bible did not have exact meanings in all the different languages spoken back then; nearly all of the Old Testament were written in Hebrew, some of it was written in Aramaic. Aramaic was the spoken language used during Jesus's time, however, all of the New Testament was written in Greek. I know this seems complicated but it really isn't.

"The Hebrew written language used twenty-two letters in their alphabet all of them consonants, no vowels. In Hebrew there was no separation between words as we read today. Let's suppose for a minute that we came across a word with the consonants 'P' and 'L' when trying to read a passage in Hebrew. Now it was up to each reader to know exactly what was written by just knowing where to place the vowels in each word to understand their sacred writing. One person might think the word used was 'Paul' and someone else might decipher it as being 'pull', then to even complicate matters even more, they didn't use any capitalized letters to show us the use of proper nouns such as someone's name, or the beginning of new sentences or paragraphs.

"Each subsequent language was translated the best it could be with each language having its own set of difficulties, the classical Greek language of the upper class was quite different from the Greek language used by the common people both written and spoken. Abby, can you see how one person translated the word kill and someone else read it as murder when the overall subject line was speaking about taking someone's life?

I turned to the book of Exodus, finding the relevant passages I wanted to share with Abby and found a note that I had written in the margin, *original translation was "tablets of the covenant"*—the ten commandants covers 17 verses and covers 14 dictates—must be followed. I continued on by saying, "Sweetheart, throughout history the ten commandments has been drastically reduced by abbreviating the verses to help people memorize the importance of God's commands. For the most part the full original text have been omitted which leads to even greater confusion."

Abby asked, "But isn't there something in the Bible about not changing anything, ya know, like adding something or taking something away from the Bible?"

"Yes, there is, it in Deuteronomy 12 verse 32.

"Sweetheart," I said, "Let me continue. I want you to think about the Ten Commandments and see if you can't cross reference the counterparts as Paul suggested using 'charity', 'pure heart', 'faith unfeigned' and 'good conscience.' Look at both lists and see if you can tell how they must criss-cross one another. No Other Gods Beside Me, worship Images, bear false witness, remember the Sabbath day and keep it holy, honor your father and your mother, thou shall not murder, thou shall not commit adultery, thou shall not steal, thou shall not bear false witness against your neighbor, thou shalt not covet your neighbor's house. One additional point I would like to make, the Ten Commandments is divided into two categories: the first five contain the 'man-to-God' mitzvot or laws and the second five are 'man-to-man' mitzvot. Abby—think real hard and try to see how ultimately the end result of all the commandments is always…'love.'"

It's amazing I thought to myself how I could recall in such precise detail our last study, and then I finally understood how God granted mankind the power of a "sound mind."

As I stood there my mind racing a mile a minute jumping here to there, my thought processes jumped back earlier today while I was in the cafeteria thinking of Abby's spiritual growth. All of a sudden I felt a feeling of relief and comfort as if God placed his hands on my shoulders saying, "Good father; job well done my faithful servant."

I then realized that I needn't have any concerns or worries concerning Abby's spiritual growth and development.

# Chapter 9: When Hearts Listen, the Angels Sing

I knew that it shouldn't be long before LaDonna would return with Aunt Cissy; I pulled open the hanging curtain that isolated one bed from another allowing me to see them when they passed the nursing station. The coronary care intensive care unit is very strict about visitors even hospital employees. Only two visitors are allowed at any one given time and everyone is required to sign-in with no exceptions. Trying to understand the rigidity and regulations are beyond me, I've been so use to the casual easygoing atmosphere of the hospice where life continued day after day with as little restraint as possible. The regiment of the CCU/ICU will take a bit of getting use to.

Hopefully later today Dr. Questa will be able to determine if Abby will be allowed to go back to her room in the hospice, but because of her coma I haven't any idea what to expect, I'm in that gray area of what I don't know.

Until now I believed I had accepted Abby's disease, but never gave thought as to the unexpected consequence of contingencies that are a direct result of her cancer. The helplessness of watching each bodily system fail one after another, watching my daughter diminish from a peppy robust healthy young girl ten years of age to a frail withered atrophied body barely twelve, decomposing right before my eyes is almost more than I can handle. It was the disease that prompted her sudden heart failure; it will also be the disease that will be responsible for Abby's eternal sleep.

Today I almost lost my daughter, I must accept the fact that tomorrow I might.

No parent is immune to the havoc and despair that cancer has upon their child. There is no way to avoid the many trials and hardships in life; it's a fact, bad things happen to good people every day without regard to position in life, I know this.

To believe in God, one must have faith that he loves and provides all things for man's ultimate good with a useful purpose and outcome. I understand God's reasoning behind opposition in all things, I also understand the difference between permitting and causing evil to befall mankind. God has permitted man to have a temporary experience with evil, so that all will come to know firsthand the contrast between living righteously or self-serving in self-absorbed disobedience.

I have tried to rationalize and justify Abby's medical condition as also being part of God's eternal plan of salvation, possibly to touch someone's heart that may have become lost or strayed, possibly a worker here in the hospital. Then again, some events in life are what they are, circumstantial, and there is no point in searching for explanations for them. I must keep myself focused in prayer not allowing the negative "mind talk" prompted by "Satan the Great Deceiver", to overtake my weakened thought processes implanting destructive ideas that God is to blame for allowing bad things to happen to a good people.

At some point in everyone's life regardless of how "naughty or nice" we each may be, natural occurrences happen that may be deplorable; we lose a loved one as in Abby's case, our best friend commits the unpardonable sin of suicide, our spouse runs off with another, the beloved family pet is run over by a car, there are thousands of examples of negative mind play used by the 'Prince of Darkness' to grab hold of a floundering soul.

Throughout the years I explained to Abby that man by his very nature could not stand alone. When Abby was five years old, I purchased a sonnet that was embedded in the fabric as a tapestry. I thought it to be perfect wall hanging to decorate her bedroom. She and I spent months memorizing its verses; it was entitled "Footprints in the Sand." I can't recall the author, but, the meaning has always been quite clear. It was about moments of growth in a person's life. It depicted how we each sustain not only ourselves, but others. It ultimately showed how God in his very essence sustains each one of us. I only pray that Abby's death can do the same.

Life is a conflict from birth to the moment of our death. It is only through this struggle of choosing the right that we forge an unbreakable bond with our Father in Heaven.

My own life has been blessed in so many ways. I'm grateful that I didn't have the problems with my daughter that so many parents have; I didn't have to contend with the worry over drugs, over disrespect, over rebellion and conflict in her pre-teen years. I'm grateful that Abby not only has a heart of gold, but compassionate about life in general. I'm grateful that for the most part; she has made quality choices and recognized love with respect and honor. I'm so grateful for the invisible hand of God protecting her night and day.

I only pray that I will remain thankful after she is gone; so often is the case that grieving parents tend to place blame on God after their loss. As strong as my faith is I'm only human and at times show my back-side, I pray that God forgive me for my weaknesses of any irreverence and disrespect I may disclose or reveal.

I stood there leaning against the side-rails of Abby's hospital bed tears falling from my eyes and spoke to my daughter saying, "Sweetheart, I don't know if you can hear and understand what I am about to say, but you have to be strong, you have to wake-up! You just can't die on me now, there's so much I still have to say, so much more you still need to know. But just in case you don't—I want you to know that as your earthy father I'm so grateful that I was able to share in your loving spirit that I will hold in my heart for all time and eternity."

At that moment I noticed LaDonna and Aunt Cissy standing at the foot of Abby's bed. I had no idea how long they had been there, or if they had overheard my comments to Abby. My eyes had been closed tightly lost in thought and I didn't see them approach.

Aunt Cissy spoke saying, "Matthew, we didn't mean to over-hear you, but it is indeed quite possible that Abby can hear and understand everything we are saying. Dr. Questa suggests that we talk to Abby; it might help her regain consciousness. Sometimes patients can be cognizance fully aware of their surroundings. Of course, there is no way of knowing. Abby's in a deep unconsciousness; one thing in her favor is that she is responsive to reflex stimulus, indicating that her nerve receptor's are active. All we can do is hope."

LaDonna stepped around the bed placing her hand on my shoulder and whispered, "She has a better than fifty-fifty chance pulling out of this. Generally speaking, the longer she stays asleep the greater her chance for survival. The body is allowing itself to heal without the interruptions and added stress of being awake. Come Matthew, we need to go now. The floor nurse needs to come in and readjust the monitor. Matthew, we need to go. Doctor Questa has only authorized ten minutes an hour for right now. The nurses will talk to her calling her by name. If she can hear, she will respond eventually. Believe me. Please, let's go please."

LaDonna took me by the hand and led me out of the intensive care unit. As we were leaving, a nurse walked-in right behind us and closed the curtain surrounding Abby's bed.

As we were about to sit down in the waiting room, Aunt Cissy reappeared holding a cup of coffee. "Here, Matthew, sit down and drink this," she said, "You need to calm down and pull yourself together. There is absolutely nothing that you can do, let someone carry the weight for awhile. Abby has a strong constitution and if it's the will of God—she'll pull through this. I've arranged to keep her room in tact for the time being. LaDonna, take him back to Abby's room and have him lay down for a while. Don't say one word, just do as I ask. Matthew, you'll feel better, believe me. Look, I'll stay up here for awhile, if there are any changes, I'll come get you. Besides, you have at least an hour before Dr. Questa will allow you to see Abby again anyway."

What I didn't know at the time was that the coffee Aunt Cissy had given me had a sedative in it. The next thing I knew, nine hours had passed before I awoke. When I opened my eyes, LaDonna was sitting next to the bed, sitting in the same chair where I had spend many a sleepless night. She told me that Abby's condition had improved; her vital signs were much stronger than Dr. Questa had even anticipated.

"I knew I was tired," I said, "But had no idea how exhausted I must have been to have slept for so long."

"Tired and stressed out," LaDonna added, "That's the reason Aunt Cissy had Dr. Jenkins prescribe a sedative. She knew you would not leave the ICU any other way, so she spiked your coffee."

"She did what?" I remarked.

LaDonna didn't say another word; she has learned to read me like a book—allowing me the space to come to terms and regain my composure knowing full well that I would be outraged with what Aunt Cissy after what she had done. What if Abby had regained consciousness and I wasn't there? What if she had done so, and then died while I was sleeping? I stood to my feet and managed to slip into my loafers, reached over to grab a windbreaker hanging on the back of a chair, and headed for the door.

"Matthew, where do you think your going?" LaDonna asked.

"I'm going to see Abby. I never should have allowed myself to go to sleep. She needs me, I know she does. Are you coming?" I asked.

"Can't you give yourself a few minutes to wake-up?" LaDonna blurted out.

"No, I can't! I have to go. Now, are you coming or not?" I said.

"Matthew, just calm-down, please. Aunt Cissy meant well, you needed some rest; you were turning into a basket case. Besides, if you allow your health to fail, you couldn't be any help to anyone let alone Abby. You have no right to be upset or angry with anyone," said LaDonna.

"Okay, whatever. What's done is done, I need to go! I just need to see Abby!" I said.

As I opened the door I stopped half-way in my tracks having instantly thought about what I had said and the manner in which I said it. I turned around and apologized saying, "LaDonna—I'm sorry I didn't mean to be so harsh, I'm not really angry at anyone, I'm far more concerned with my daughter than being upset with Aunt Cissy. I realize that no harm was intended," I said.

"Wait up, Matthew," LaDonna said, "I'm going with you."

As LaDonna and I were waiting for the elevator she looked over at me and said, "Matthew, after we see Abby, we both really need to clean up a bit. Don't you agree? I don't know about you but I'm famished, neither one of us have eaten anything since early yesterday morning. Let's grab something to eat after we check-in with Abby, doesn't breakfast sound good?"

I actually hadn't given it any thought until then. LaDonna was right; I must have looked a sight. I was unshaven, hadn't brushed my teeth, my hair was uncombed; I slept in my clothes, in reality I must have looked like someone who had just crawled out of the homeless shelter. But at that exact moment it just didn't matter to me, my appearance was one thing; Abby's life is totally another. I needed to be with my daughter even if I wasn't the best dressed father on the floor.

On the elevator I was thinking that my mind hadn't cleared from the sleep. I felt somewhat drugged and couldn't remember when I had that much undisturbed rest. I also thought how good it actually felt as if the weight of the world had been removed from my shoulders for just a few hours. I can't remember when my mind was so void. After thinking it over—actually I'm grateful for Aunt Cissy's prescribed remedy of health, unorthodox as it may have been given.

As LaDonna and I entered the ICU, Dr. Jenkins was sitting behind the nurses' desk writing out his doctor's orders. "Matthew," he said, "Abby is doing as well as expected and we couldn't hope for any more. Her vitals are improving, her color is coming back and her output is good."

"Thank you Dr. J, can LaDonna and I go in now?" I asked.

"Sure, but remember you can only stay a few minutes," he said.

I stood close to the head of her bed placing my hand on her forehead and noticed that she was running a fever. The fever gave me little concern, at least she was alive, still fighting showing me she wasn't ready to let go, not just yet.

"Matthew, we have to go. Our time is up," LaDonna said.

"I know," I said, as I leaned over and kissed Abby on her forehead. Walking out of the room I prayed silently asking God to protect her until I returned. Within seconds I realized how asinine my prayer must have sounded, as if I could protect her any better than God could. In my mind I looked up to the heavens and asked God to forgive my petition apologizing for my arrogance.

We left the ICU/CCU deciding that we both needed a little personal grooming time; I would return to Abby's room to shower and shave as LaDonna could go the nurse's lounge to grab a quick shower and fresh change of clothes.

It's strange, but Abby's room in the hospice seemed more like a hotel room than a place where one goes to die. The room itself was small, just large enough to hold a hospital bed, one night stand, a dresser and chair and portable over-the-bed tray. When I brought in my recliner, the room really felt cramped. It had a three-quarter size bathroom with a sit-down shower stall and the addition of stainless steel handrails placed where one might imagine a patient might need them.

LaDonna said that she would call me when she was ready. I knew I had a little time; it always takes a woman longer to bathe and dress than it does a man. I immediately grabbed a shower, washed my hair and dressed. Having gotten dressed I realized that I had forgotten to shave. I never shower and then shave; I have always shaved before I stepped into the shower. I removed my shirt and started to lather my face when I heard LaDonna return.

"Hi, I'm back," I heard her say in a muffled tone as she entered the room. "Listen, I ran into Aunt Cissy and she said she would join us for breakfast in about ten minutes. Is that all right with you? Matthew, can you hear me? Are you okay?" she asked.

I opened the bathroom door and asked what she had said. I told her the water was running and I couldn't exactly make out what she was saying.

"I'll be finished in a few minutes," I said.

I opened the door so we could at least understand what the other might be saying. To my surprise, she stood in the doorway and watched me as I finished shaving. With my head tilted back, I could see her partial reflection out of the corner of my eye in the mirror. She was leaning against the doorjamb with a look of fascination.

"I've never watched a man shave before," she said, "as a floor nurse, I shaved male patients who were in my care. I know it sounds silly, but it's true. Since I've never been married and just for the record not that I have to say anything, but, I just want you to know I have never spent the night with any man hence I have never seen any man shave on his own accord. So the opportunity was never there. I hope you don't mind my watching."

"No, not at all, LaDonna, I don't mind," I said. "In a way, it is somewhat flattering. This may not be the time, but you and I do need to sit down and have a long talk. There are so many things we have never discussed," I said.

"Anything out of the ordinary we need to talk about?" LaDonna asked. "We are much to close to have any withholds. Listen, I'm going to call Aunt Cissy and tell her we need a few minutes more before we catch-up with her."

"LaDonna—nothing to serious, just talk," I said. "It's nothing to worry about, in fact I'm looking forward to our making time for one another. I mean after what we went through today, don't you agree that maybe, just maybe we need to, I mean maybe I need to be open and honest with you."

LaDonna stood there with a look of apprehension and uncertainty on her face.

"Look, I'm not very good at this sort of thing," I said. "I don't even know if I know the right words. It's been so long since—well, when I awoke seeing you sitting by the bed, I knew that the time had come that I needed to tell you exactly how I might be feeling—about you as a person, as a woman."

LaDonna lowered her head and in a child-like soft spoken manner asked, "Is this something I may not want to hear?"

Immediately I responded by saying, "NO, NO, LaDonna, nothing like that, you've been a real comfort for me for a long time and I don't know what I would have done without you."

"Really!" she exclaimed.

I answered by saying, "I've known for a long time how you feel about me, Aunt Cissy and I spoke about it some time ago and Abby has done everything in her powers to assure that you and I got together somehow. I'm not stupid; I've been able to read between the lines. It's all the little things that you have done since the first time we met. The afghan, for an instance, I knew that you really knitted it for me. Now don't deny it, please don't say anything just let me finish. Isn't it amazing that the afghan is the perfect width and length for my recliner and in my favorite color too. You also knew that my favorite woman's perfume was 'Joy', and you made it a point to see to it that it had just the right amount of rose fragrance sprayed on the wool. There have been so many other ways and incidents that a blind man couldn't stumble over.

"What really, really made me realize that I cared and had feelings for you too, was the conversation that you and Abby had, while you thought I was asleep yesterday. You were so concerns about me as a man, and you were willing to wait until the time was just right. I guess, what I am trying to say is that the time could never be more appropriate than now. LaDonna, I've been afraid for a long time not wanting to step out of my comfort zone for fear of—I suppose a great many things. What I'm trying to say is that I love you, and I want us to share the rest of our together, whatever that may be. You have opened up your heart to me on more than one occasion, now it's my turn. LaDonna I know this isn't the most romantic of places but my feelings are real—LaDonna will you marry me?"

LaDonna leaped to her feet without thought and said, "Matthew, if you only knew how I have dreamed about this moment. And yes, funny as it may sound even in my fantasies you did propose here at the hospital in Abby's room. Of course I accept—I love you too, but you already knew that didn't you."

"Matthew are you sure this is what you're feeling? With everything that's going on with Abby, are you sure that you want to marry me?" LaDonna questioned.

"Yes, LaDonna, I'm sure. I have prayed about it and believe me, I don't take marriage lightly. Marriage is much more than the joining of two people sharing whatever life has to offer. It is a state of mind, a spiritual enrichment that goes far beyond human boundaries. Marriage is a gift from God, established with certain responsibilities that surpass mankind's ostensive laws. God never intended man to live alone in isolation without a helpmate, nor break the covenant sworn to; he sanctified marriage as a blessing instituted for all time and eternity. I know that if we should marry, we would indeed have his blessing."

LaDonna looked into my eyes and said, "Oh—Matthew, I too have prayed for this moment. I have always wanted to marry, but the right man never came along, I resolved myself to a life of service helping others. Sometimes God has a way of touching our souls when we least suspect it. The first day that I met you and Abby, I knew then that we were destined to be together. There were times before we met that I had to pray for patience and endurance, thinking that my time would never come. Now it's here and I'm speechless. I love you so Matthew, and yes, I would be honored to be your wife."

"LaDonna, I have to ask. How did you know that our lives were meant to be shared together?" I asked.

"Matthew, if you were anyone else I wouldn't be able to say this but knowing how strong your believe system is I can honestly say— an angel told me. I had an overwhelming desire to be near you and Abby. The messages we receive from angel's can be as simple as an indescribable feeling that comes over us, like the one I experienced the day we met. Angels work out of sight for the most part but I guarantee that if we listen or look hard enough the signs of their presence will always be there. I've been blessed to have witnessed their work on several occasion, they're always present always there to guide and protect when called upon," LaDonna said.

At that moment, we both knew that the hand of God was upon us, as we kissed passionately for the very first time.

Without warning, the door opened and Aunt Cissy entered. There could be no doubt in her mind, seeing the two of us holding each other in a tender embrace, what she was thinking. I don't know who was more embarrassed, she or us. Immediately we felt the need to give an explanation, but before either one of us could speak, Aunt Cissy walked over and gave us a big hug, saying, "I know the angel's in heaven are surely crying tears of joy this very moment for the love I feel in this room. God bless you both."

I felt such peace of mind unlike ever before, my only regret was that Abby wasn't there to share the moment.

"Well now," Aunt Cissy said, "are we still going to breakfast, or has that changed too? Listen, let's go eat you can tell me the who, what and where, the why I already know. The why is because God wants the two of you together, nothing else matter, now does it," she said.

On the way down to the cafeteria, LaDonna and Aunt Cissy couldn't keep their eyes from passing secretive looks to one another. Neither one of them said anything, but it was obvious as to what they were thinking. Between my daughter, Aunt Cissy and LaDonna, I didn't stand a chance; especially with the hand of God as their guiding light.

While the three of us sat and ate our meal, I could tell that Aunt Cissy had something on her mind. I didn't know what it was, but I could tell she had something she wanted to say. Finally the suspense was getting the best of me, deciding just to come right out and ask her.

"Aunt Cissy," I said. "Is everything all right? I mean, I have a feeling that you would like to say something. If there is, it's okay, go ahead. Say anything that you would like to. Are you concerned about the relationship that LaDonna and I have developed?"

"No quite the opposite," she remarked. "If anything I'm delighted that the two of you found one another. But your right, I do have concerns. Not about you and LaDonna, but for Abby. What I'm about to say, may not sound appropriate to you right now."

"Aunt Cissy, it's all right, say what you like. I promise I won't take it the wrong way," I said.

"Very well Matthew," Aunt Cissy said, "We never did finish our talk about 'eternal perceptual vision' and I know you didn't really want to hear some of the things that I have to say. However, it's more important now then ever before. You and LaDonna never could have found each other if God didn't approve. Do you agree?"

"Yes, I agree," I said.

"Do you also agree that Abby's life is now in the hands of God?" she asked.

"Yes, I agree as well," I repeated.

"Well then, there is something else I have to tell you. Remember you were under the impression that Abby's dreams just seemed to vanish and fade away. That simply wasn't the case. Both LaDonna and I promised Abby that we would never mention to you that the dreams she was having only escalated, not diminished. She was able to keep them from you. She knew that you resisted the whole concept of 'eternal perceptual vision'."

LaDonna joined in, saying, "Sweetheart, try and understand, Abby made us both promise that neither one of us would ever say anything to you about her dreams."

"I fully understand what you're saying," I said. "But, what does her dream have to do with us right now? I mean, I just don't understand."

Aunt Cissy looked over to LaDonna who was holding my hand and said, "LaDonna, I'll tell him. We know for a fact that the moment Abby learns the good news about you and LaDonna, she plans on returning to the 'veil of life' and give up her spirit. She had told me more times than I care to remember how she wouldn't leave your side, until she knew you and LaDonna were together."

"Aunt Cissy, LaDonna, can the two of you hear exactly what you are saying?" I asked. "If we were anywhere near the psych ward the two of you would be committed. I'm sorry; I just can't comprehend the coming and going in and out of the spirit world."

"Abby knew that's the way you felt. That was her reasoning behind the promise," declared Aunt Cissy.

"Listen kids, I need to make a telephone call. I'll be back soon," said Aunt Cissy.

"LaDonna, I still don't understand. What am I missing? Why the grave concern? Can't you please explain it to me?" I said.

LaDonna looked at me and said, "Honey, give me your hand."

I reached over the table placing my hand in LaDonna's. She held it tight and said, "How does it feel holding my hand?"

"It feels good," I said.

"What else?" asked LaDonna.

I looked to LaDonna as if to say, I still don't get it.

"What do you mean what else?" I asked.

"I mean explain to me what you're feeling," LaDonna said.

"I like it—It's nice, it's comfortable. Holding your hands just reinforces what you and I both share," I said.

"There you have it Matthew. Now, take the same concept of holding my hand and direct it to Abby standing in the presence of the Holy Trinity. Right now, she is in the threshold of crossing over from the secular to the spiritual. Abby's desire to cross over is nothing more than that same love reinforcement for her Father in Heaven. The concerns we have are absolute, Abby made it quite clear that once she is certain that you and I have finally made a connection she is planning to reach out for the hand of the 'angel of death' to be escorted to God," LaDonna explained.

It was just a matter of minutes when Aunt Cissy returned saying, "I called upstairs to the ICU, there's still no change. I'm waiting for Dr. Questa to get back with me. I have a question he needs to answer."

I just sat there in silence, thinking over everything that LaDonna explained. I don't claim to know it all especially where the ways of God are concerned. It's true that I have never accepted the idea of 'eternal perceptual vision' or what other may call "near death experience." Yet, what if it is true?

I realize what we don't understand is what we fear the most; I am also aware that fear does not come from Lord God. Somehow, some way Aunt Cissy and LaDonna have reached a level of knowing something that I have yet to understand or experience. I have given this whole "EVP" issue great thought since the first time Aunt Cissy mentioned it to me. One night a few months ago while Abby was fast asleep, I looked-up every reference in the Bible that spoke of angel's to refresh my memory. I cannot deny that I found several endorsements as to their earthly appearances. Throughout the entire Bible stories have been told giving reference as to their mission here on earth, and I suppose that could even include those who are dying. I asked myself why I was having a hard time accepting this concept, I wondered. If only it were written somewhere in the scriptures than I'm sure I could find acceptance based on faith is nothing else.

After Aunt Cissy sat back down, LaDonna explained that she had disclosed Abby's intentions to me.

"Matthew, remember that God speaks to each of us differently," said Aunt Cissy. "Let's go up and see Abby now, all we can do is hope and pray."

As we walked into the ICU, Aunt Cissy pulled LaDonna back allowing me to go in first by myself. I stood at the foot of Abby's bed silently asking God to give me strength and understanding to allow me not only to accept his will but to yield to his needs and desires.

Not knowing if Abby will ever recover from her deep-rooted unconsciousness I also have my doubts if I will be able to tell her of LaDonna and I having enjoined our hearts. Only God knows if she is mindful of her surroundings; if she doesn't understand me—so be it, if she does however it will allow her the freedom to move on if she so chooses having found the peace of mind she has requested for such a long time. But before I say anything I want her moved back into her room at the hospice. I walked around the side of the bed and noticed that the last medical I.V. had been removed, leaving only one of "Dextrose 5% Water with Nutrients" for her nourishment. I felt like an idiot for having not noticed it before. I picked up Abby's hand and stood there in silence, thinking of my regrets. "Abby," I whispered softly, "sweetheart, I know that you are about to leave, and where your going, I can't even imagine or conceive the beauty and splendor. As deep as my love is for God, I can't even comprehend the magnificence of standing in his presence. Darling, in many ways I envy the journey you are about to take."

I don't know what made me think about it, probably a little nudge from my guardian angel, but I remembered having an old photograph of Abigail tucked away between my drivers license and social security card in my wallet. The photograph was tattered and worn, a little faded with a yellowish tint, covered with lines and creases from age having been in my wallet all these years. I reached across the bed and clasped Abby's hands together placing the photograph between them.

"Sweetheart," I said, "I wish you could see this—I have a photograph of your mother, if I remember correctly it was taken when she was about six months pregnant with you. At the time we didn't know if you were a boy or a girl, it didn't matter to us as long as you were healthy, we were just grateful that we were given the opportunity to have you. I wish you could have known your mother; she was a very beautiful lady. I know that throughout the years people have told you that you looked a lot like me, that may be so— but, I think you resemble your mother far more than me.

"You have so many of her ways and characteristics, she loved life in the same way you always have, and she even liked butter popcorn just as much as you do. Your tenderness and compassion is identical to that of your mother's, a soft side with a heart of gold, there are times that I can look at you and see your mother plain as day. Your mother had a whimsical side that could make me laugh to tears. She was a woman of great courage, quite logical most of the time but had her moments when driven by impulse and spontaneity. In all of our years today not once did I ever see her cry, she used to tease me unmercifully when we would sit-down to watch a movie together especially if it were on the Hallmark channel, asking if I had enough Kleenex before the movie started knowing full well somewhere within the storyline I would begin to cry over some silly little sad thing, but then you already know that, don't you. Your mother always insisted on saving the last portion regardless of what it might be for me even though I told her it wasn't necessary. It didn't manner if it was the last chicken leg left over from dinner or the last slice of pie, especially apple pie. Somehow she came to believe that apple pie was my favorite, that's when I reminded her that apple pie was in fact your favorite; she had the cutest way of wrinkling her nose and upper lip saying 'oh yeah you're right' laughing softly with little restraint as she began to eat it.

"Your mother was definitely one of a kind, I suppose that's the main reason I never had the desire to be with someone else knowing for sure that I would never find another woman like your mom."

When I exited the ICU, LaDonna and Aunt Cissy were sitting in the waiting room, I explained to them what I had done and asked that they help me see to it that the photo remain with Abby, until the end.

"Now, Matthew, let's not talk about the end just yet. Let's just hope for the best," Aunt Cissy said.

"Dr. Jenkins came by when you were in with Abby," said LaDonna. "He said that Dr. Questa was well pleased with Abby's condition. He also said that she is showing signs that are favorable to her coming out of the coma."

"Aunt Cissy," I said, "Can you find out if Questa and Jenkins will allow Abby to be moved back to her room in the hospice? I've decided I want to tell her even in her comatose state about LaDonna and me, but she must be in surroundings she feels comfortable with. She has actually considered her room to be her home."

Aunt Cissy reached over and gave me a pat on my cheek and said, "Why don't the two of you go for a walk, step outside and get a breath of fresh air. There is no reason to sit here and worry about things we can't change anyway. Now go, I'll know where you are if need be. I'll contact the doctors to see where we stand. Matthew, I can see no reason they should object. Now the two of you go."

LaDonna and I agreed that a breath of fresh air would be nice. Stepping outside the hospital the weather was pleasant and quite enjoyable. As we walked way around the grounds, LaDonna and I spoke very little. I think she was giving me space for thought.

"Matthew," LaDonna asked, "can we talk?"

"Sure, talk about what?" I asked.

"About everything," LaDonna replied. "You're so quiet, is there something I can do to help? I am a good listener you know. Please allow me to be there for you as you have been for Abby."

"Oh, LaDonna, I guess I'm just in my own little world, trying to sort things out. I just want to cry, but I can't. I wish I could make things better, but I can't do that either," I said.

"Are you okay with us? LaDonna asked.

"Sweetheart—I'm sorry. Yes, I'm fine with us. In fact right now I'm finding I'm gaining a great deal of strength just being near you. Honey…it's been a long time since I called anybody honey except Abby. Please understand, our relationship is new, it's exciting, and it's wonderful. I wish I only had more energy to put into it. I wish we could go out and have a nice dinner somewhere, go to a movie or see a play. You deserve better than what I am able to give you right now. I'm feeling like a failure as a man, and I don't know why," I said.

"Sweetheart—now, doesn't that sound good, my calling you sweetheart?" LaDonna asked.

I nodded my head as if to say yes.

"I know exactly what you're feeling," she continued. "You have no need to beat yourself up for the emotions your feeling inside. A little while ago you were thinking of your life with Abigail when you placed her picture into Abby's hands recalling what your life was like for the two of you back then. Now here we are, you and I, walking hand in hand, do you think that maybe, just maybe you might be feeling a bit ambivalent or guilty? Matthew, I'm not trying to play psychologist, even if I could, I wouldn't because I love you. Just remember I'll always be here for you, until the day I die."

"LaDonna, that's so sweet of you," I said. "Thank you for being so understanding, and you could be right. I must admit I was thinking of a contrast between the two of you, but not in the way you might suppose. I wasn't thinking of any likeness or resemblance between the two of you as people, but in a spiritual sense. I'm grateful that the only two women in my life understood how important my beliefs are. I'm also questioning the nature of who I am, not my ability to love provide or care for you; but in my own priorities. I know that each scenario is different, but doesn't it strike you a bit odd that at this very moment my daughter is upstairs in a hospital room fighting for her life and I'm out here taking a leisurely stroll? It doesn't seem right somehow."

"Matthew, there a bench in the garden just around that rose acacia tree—let's sit down for a few minutes, there are some things I would like to say and walking with you in this moonlight is throwing off my concentration." LaDonna giggled. "I've always daydreamed of taking a moonlit promenade with the man I loved but somehow I don't think this scenario came into my fantasy."

We sat down and I pointed out, "LaDonna, you amaze me, I'm honestly impressed, your knowing the name of that bush right there."

"Matthew, I finally have the courage to have this talk with you so please just sit there and listen. I love you and because I do I just can't keep silent any longer. I'm trying to find just the right words to say but to be perfectly candid I really don't know how you are going to respond. So please let me say what I must before you make comment or judgment one way or another, alright.

"First of all—fact is fact; Abby is not fighting for her life as you might think, her body has simply shutdown and as sad as it may be it is probably for the best thing at this point. Her body is trying to regain strength on its own, and that's good, she's also feeling no pain.

"Now, it's not an easy thing to tell someone you love that their whole life is in disarray, everything for you right now is so chaotic. You're being pushed and pulled from every direction all at once and our validating our commitment hadn't made it any easier on you either. When was the last night you had a good-nights rest? When was the last time you were home—you don't even remember, do you? Matthew my dear, I'm trying to find out just where exactly I fit in, what I can do to help other than simply standing by your side.

"I also think you're blaming and reprimanding yourself for things you can't control; what I really think is deep-down you are actually blaming yourself for Abigail's death, after all if she hadn't gotten pregnant maybe she would be here today, but remember—neither would Abby have been born. Subsequently I think perhaps on a subconscious level you are looking to blame someone for Abby's cancer, and since you can't find anyone else to blame you look to yourself.

"Matthew as soon as you give yourself permission to forgive yourself for what you may be feeling and come to terms with the idea that bad things just happen to the ones we love, you and I can go on with our lives. You no more caused their deaths than I can walk on water!

"You talk about priorities and putting things in their proper place, well, you're not God and you can't save the entire world. You're not responsible for the problems of the world. And another thing, you didn't seek out to fall in love with me, it just happened. Matthew, you're the most giving caring man I have ever known always thinking of others and never yourself. But you do have one fault, you place blame on yourself for things you have no control over. Look, you have to allow me to be honest with you, you may not like what I have to say, but you do have to listen. If we are going to be married I must have the right to express my opinions. Don't you agree?

"All that I'm saying is that you are much too hard on yourself; you need to lighten-up a little, give yourself permission to be human. You can't give anymore than what you're capable of, and right now, you're running on empty.

"Matthew there's one more little thing I need to say—well actually we may need to talk about; Abby swore me to secrecy not to reveal what I am about to tell you and I'm only telling you this so as not to have any more secrets from you. When you first showed Abby the album with snapshots and photos of her mother, how did she seem to you?"

"Okay I guess. Why?" I answered, "but didn't we already have this conversation with your telling me what Abby's intentions are?"

"Well, yes and no," LaDonna said. "I want to be able to tell you the rest of what we were speaking about early on this evening. Didn't you ever stop to think or question why she suddenly stopped having those terrifying dreams and wasn't afraid any longer? If you recall— she simply stopped talking about it…to you that is. Matthew, Abby wasn't afraid of having dreams she was concerned with their meaning and feared what she didn't understand as a child; strangers hovering over her. She had been programmed by you, her school and every adult she has ever known telling her since she took her first baby steps to be apprehensive of strangers, at first as a child her dreams were threatening, dark and menacing. It wasn't until it was explained to her '*by her mother*' that her dreams were really a natural occurrence leading from this life into the next, that she was able to understand and accept the will of God.

"Matthew, Abby confided in me the very next day after you first showed her the photo album telling me that the lady in her reoccurring dreams, the one always standing in the center looked just like the pictures of her mother. At first I didn't say anything, but she must have been thinking about it quite a bit, because a few days later she told me she absolutely knew in fact that it was indeed her birth mother Abigail. She, Aunt Cissy and I spoke about her dreams whenever we were given the chance when you were out of the room. All of the little errands we asked to do was primarily to give us some alone time without your interference. Abby tried to explain to me what she meant and felt saying it was a 'feeling of nice', she went on to say that although her mother wasn't able to be here with her physically—she also knew that her mother never left her side, that she had always been with her in spirit.

"Abby also went on to say that her visits with her mother were almost a daily occurrence, apparently Abigail explained to her about stepping through the veil walking toward the light, the light being an angelic host to guide her transition into the spirit realm. Abigail assured Abby that she too would be there awaiting her appointed time. I didn't know what to make of it by myself so I called Aunt Cissy and she came running down to give comfort to both Abby and I. That's the reason Aunt Cissy has been so adamant about your understanding what you perceive as a near death experience, just in case somewhere along the way, you were indeed confronted with its reality."

I stood up from where we were sitting reached down grasping both of LaDonna's hands looked her deep into her eyes and said,

"Thank you darling, sometimes we need someone with a fresh perception from the outside looking-in to hit us over the head with a brick reaffirming who we really are. I agree with you, sometimes we get so wrapped-up with everything going on in our lives that we fail to see the forest for the trees. As far as Abby's spiritual enlightenment is concerned—what can I say? I don't doubt anything that she has told you and she apparently knows a great deal more about it than I do. At least now, knowing this much, I have little choice but to abide by her wishes. As soon as we can arrange to have her moved back to the hospice if you would stand by my side I plan on telling her that in the near future you and I will marry. Either way it will be her decision—frankly if it were me, I have little doubt that I would go anywhere else except to my celestial reward. Once again—thank you and don't ever be afraid to talk to me about anything ever again, okay." Are you ready to go back up yet?"

As LaDonna and I were approaching the main entrance to the hospital, I looked up to the heavens and silently gave thanks for this special gift of companionship and a new life to look forward to, a new life with a mate who has no qualms of speaking her mind when need be.

# Chapter 10: Standing Beside the Still Waters

Walking back into the hospital with LaDonna by my side would have been something Abby would have given anything to see. Thinking back over this past year I wasn't surprised to find the many instances how LaDonna had become such an influence into our lives, both Abby's and mine, and slowly over time our relationship flowered ever so quietly in the background blossoming into a vibrant rose of beauty of what it is today. Without my realizing it God had placed the love of a good woman directly beside me who initially had in a very platonic way given me strength easing my burden of Abby's condition, now that unemotional phlegmatic woman has given me a love I never thought possible.

Our newly found relationship is as strong if not stronger than many marriages I have known, I suppose because of the situational gravity of our lives. LaDonna has a way of reinforcing my belief system allowing me look at life not only as a man—but a man of God, sharing a spiritual dimension unlike anything I can remember when I was married to Abigail as a young man in my early twenties. Over the years I have changed, acquired life experiences and knowledge unavailable to me back then. I know it isn't fair by comparison because no two element or people are ever the same, in my youth I'm sure I was foolish in many ways, hopefully I have become a great deal wiser.

Upon entering the elevator we encountered Dr. Jenkins who said that he was on his way up to check on Abby. "Matthew—LaDonna, are you two available this afternoon after Dr. Questa makes his rounds for a brief consultation?" he asked. "How about 3:00 PM, in the conference room on the second floor?"

"Sure, Mark. It isn't like our schedules have conflicting appointments," I replied.

The three of us walked in together to the CCU/ICU and to our astonishment we found Dr. Roger Mendinhall, a neurologist standing over her Abby's bedside.

"Mark, that didn't take you very long, what, were you standing right outside the door?" he said. "I was already up here when Nurse Jeffries asked me to look on your patient."

"Did they page me?" asked Mr. J.

Nurse Jeffries indicated that she had by a simple nod of her head, within seconds Dr. J's pager was beeping.

"Mark as you can see this young girl is regaining non-subjective clinical nerve activity although still unconscious. Mark, has she been unable to respond to external stimuli the entire time? It has been my experience in cases such as this that it's just a matter of time before she regains consciousness," said Dr. Mendinhall, adding, "were you ever able to determine what precipitated her unconsciousness?"

"Roger, your guess is still as good as mine. If you only knew how strong willed this patient is, despite having passed her clinical estimate of survival prediction by a margin of 2.1 months even with a standing DNR she refuses to die, she's a hospice patient of mine; I delivered her some twelve years ago, feisty little thing she was, early delivery and underweight, now we're here just waiting out whatever timetable there is. Yesterday she fell into a cardiac shutdown and recessed into her current state stemming from what Questa and his staff indicated as a calcium magnesium electrolyte disturbance, a class IV stage B CHF and for some unknown reason fell into a coma," replied Dr. J, "I appreciate your help and opinion, have your office fax over a referral form and I'll sign it to submit your time for billing to the insurance company."

"Mark that awfully generous of you, however it really isn't necessary, I was already here seeing to another patient. Let me know if I can ever be of future service," said Dr. Mendinhall.

Abby's arms and legs were starting to quiver without conscious control from nerve pulsations; her body would wrench and wiggle with jerking motions as if she were in a mild seizure. I guess I must have had a perplexing look on my face because Mark spoke up and said, "Don't be concerned Matthew, this is a good thing, a very good thing. I'll get in touch with Dr. Questa and cancel our meeting for this afternoon," Mark said, "the reason we wanted to meet with you was to discuss a plan of action just in case Abby recovered from her current state and obviously it might just well happen, we'll give it a little more time. Dr. Questa and I discussed having Abby moved back to her room since she is no longer in a critical state, especially since a DNR is in effect with little else that can be done."

I know I must have had a dumbfounded look on my face. Although Mark was a good friend, he was still a doctor and has a tendency to leave us laymen in the dark. I couldn't understand how he considered her body reeling and swaying a good thing.

"Matthew, don't be alarmed. Peter and I spoke just before I ran into you on the elevator. Trust me; at that point neither he nor I were aware of her nerve cell palpitations. As her physician of record I will be the only doctor treating Abby from this point on. Let me explain this, it might make you feel better; the cerebral hemispheres of her brain function despite overly-simplistic descriptions of lateral line sensory receptors between the left-brain/ right-brain are in conflict, what that means is there are specific areas of her brain telling her body to do certain things which at present doesn't recognize due to her unconscious state. Matthew I really can't say how much if anything registers in Abby's subconscious mind right now, it's a waiting game we have no choice but to play.

"By the way you two, I heard from the hospital scuttlebutt that congratulations may be in order. Personally I think it's great, you know how I felt about Abigail and I'm sure she would agree it's about time! Have me paged if you need me, I'll be around. I'll see if I can round-up a couple of aids to get Abby moved back to her room. Tell Aunt Cissy I'll send Abby's chart back down as soon as I can make a few notes, if you would please."

Mark left without saying another word. I knew he felt half-way comfortable with Abby condition, but I didn't. When Dr. J asked about the gossip neither LaDonna nor I responded, I suppose like everyone else he could read between the lines—the looks of love are hard to mistake.

LaDonna looked at me and asked if I was alright, I responded saying, "LaDonna, I'm really trying to hold my composure, I really am, but I just don't get it. Not two hours ago just before you and I went for our walk both you and I saw Abby laying here without any movement, now her fingers and hands are twitching showing signs of possible recovery. How is this possible? I mean what else—she has already outlived the timeline we were given, do you think that maybe somehow she might wake up and we find that her cancer has gone into remission. Is that possible?"

"Matthew, my dear Matthew," LaDonna said as she put her arms around my neck and drew herself near, "Abby's body is trying to wake-up. The brain is still asleep, but her body is still receiving weak indistinct nerve impulses that are snarled and mixed-up due to her unconsciousness. So when Dr. Jenkins says that it's a good thing, believe me, it really is. Can't you see, honey; this is Abby's first step in coming back to us. Sometimes the mind and body can't always agree, and one system will try and override the other. Once the mind and body can harmonize then the tremors will stop."

"Why couldn't Mark explain it to me that way?" I asked.

"I'm sure he did, but as her father you tend to look deeper, searching for hidden prevalent factors, despite the fact they may not exist. We all have a tendency to hear only what we want to hear," LaDonna answered.

True to his word, Dr. Jenkins appeared moment later with two male hospital attendants to move Abby back down to her room on the hospice wing. The photograph of her mother that I had placed loosely between her hands was still there. Regardless of how rose-colored optimistic Dr. J may be, I still feel as if these are the last few hours of Abby's life, or maybe it's just the preparation Abby's guardian angel is putting me through.

Having lived each stage of her death beforehand from the initial shock to the fear and frustration of watching her slip away slowly has given me the strength to be able to accept her death as inevitable, yet, I still struggle with acceptance as a mortal man. I know that the divine will of God will prevail, but to embrace the act of a loved one dying is still challenging. The only true comfort I find is in the knowing that her name is written in gold, in the book of life.

LaDonna and I decided to slip-out for a few minutes to grab a quick bite of lunch down in the cafeteria while Aunt Cissy and Dr. J were getting Abby resettled. Just before we left, Aunt Cissy made it a point to tell us that when we returned she needed a few minutes of our time.

Over lunch my mind just drifting back and forth into that blank void of unknown, which I am apparently becoming quite familiar with. I can't explain it, it just a 'nothingness' that comes over me as if my mind had suddenly been wiped-clean of all data.

LaDonna reached out placing her hand in mine and gave a gentle squeeze. "Matthew, I've been thinking," she said, "now that Abby's back in her own room and hopefully can sense the peace found there, I think we need to start talking to Abby whether she responds or not. I think that by Abby hearing our voices could be a big help. I mean, let's face it, it can't hurt. Better yet, let's make her involved—we can ask her questions as if she were lucid having a clear mind capable of thinking and expressing yourself, if there's no response that okay too, but one never knows just what might happen."

I agreed wholeheartedly with LaDonna; anything was worth a try. I have prayed for just one more day, for just one more hour…maybe this was the opportunity I had pled for.

I am beginning to appreciate and cherish every moment that LaDonna and I spend together; over the years I had forgotten how pleasant a woman's company could be, especially one you're in love with. I am certain that it has become quite noticeable to all, that our interests, roles, virtues and beliefs are becoming a shared identity allowing emotional interdependence from/for one another.

I had little doubt as to what Aunt Cissy wanted to talk about; Aunt Cissy is convinced that Abby's dreams were definitely an angelic intervention. I am trying my best to accept and understand the role that spiritual messengers take when dealing with human beings, as guides and mentors. I have no doubt that they exist, I only question their presence with our knowing. There is a part of me that accepts without question the reality of their existence here on earth. As a child I was taught that angels were invisible and only transact with our lives indirectly; that they protected us, they guide us, they convey the love of God to mankind. But who am I to question the rhymes and reasons behind the scheme of angels? I for one haven't the answers.

Even Abby believes that she has had contact with angelic beings, having even made contact with her mother in spirit form somehow. All I know for certain is that God is love, the Gospel of Jesus Christ is love and the power of prayer is real, as for the rest I simply can't say right now.

"Matthew, Aunt Cissy will be here momentarily, there a fresh shirt for you to change into if you wish hanging in Abby's closet," LaDonna said.

When Aunt Cissy arrived I was in the bathroom freshening-up as suggested by LaDonna; for the life of me I wondered how she managed to retrieve a clean shirt since as far as I knew the laundry hadn't been returned.

Every few days generally twice a week Mr. Pascal from 'Pascal Cleaners and Laundry Service' would come to Abby's room and drop off the clean laundry that he had picked-up previously taking with him a bag of what needed to be cleaned, to repeat the same setting week after week. I have used Pascal for many years now, with the exception of our underwear and Abby's wash and wear jeans, each week I would drop-off and pickup at his plant on the other side of town. If it needed to be pressed, it went to Pascal's. The one chore I hate with a passion was to do the ironing. I can cook and clean with the best of them, but ironing is banned according to the 'Law of Matthew'. Pascal has been a life-saver figuratively, his making delivery here to the hospital.

When I walked out of the bathroom I asked Aunt Cissy if she felt we needed to talk elsewhere, she shrugged her shoulders as if to say 'it doesn't matter to her one way or another'. Her mood was anything but negative or as Abby would have said, 'a downer'. So I felt relieved thinking she was going to start on me once again with her 'eternal perceptual vision' theory.

"LaDonna—Matthew, sit down before I start. Frankly I want to get the information I have for you out of the way before going into other areas of concerns such as, have the two of you set a date yet?

"Well Kids, first I have news that you may consider a mixed blessing. As you know Dr. King is the chairman of the board and executive hospital administrator overseeing every department here at Mercy General, well, somehow he heard of LaDonna's choice to take a leave of absence without pay just to be near Abby; to be able to see to her patients needs regardless of the consequences to her personally. He was so impressed by her dedication not only as a nurse but as a non-medical surrogate mother who was thinking only of Abby, decided that the hospital should also do whatever it could to help as in a partnership so to speak. Dr. King and I had several discussions at great length and we think we have come-up with what could be construed as being a bit unconventional, but we agree that it's workable and not illegal—that's a joke kids, that's a joke. However, there are a few things that must be spelled-out before I can tell you anything further. First of all, LaDonna—as of tomorrow your non-paid leave of absence is revoked;..."

"WHAT?" LaDonna exclaimed. "I can't go back to the floor—I guess I just have to formally submit my termination notice."

"LaDonna, settle down—let me finish. We are not about to accept your resignation now and hopefully never. If you allow me to finish I was about to say…as of tomorrow, you are being placed on sabbatical leave with PAY for the duration of whatever timeframe is necessary. Think of it as a medical furlough, now there are only two conditions. The first condition; you must document Abby's entire medical treatment plan going back to day one from the very beginning; under the auspices of medical research, to warrant continuation of your salary. Dr. King also agreed to a retroactive reinstatement since you first began your leave of absence so you'll be getting a nice fat check for back pay; after all the years of your dedicated service here at the hospital—it really is only right.

"Condition number two; LaDonna, since you will be documenting Abby's care, her nutritional I.V. must not be allowed to run-dry or become obstructed, Matthew, we have to take these precautions to make the legal-eagles happy, covering ourselves since you have signed her right to die affidavit. Now don't jump to conclusions, no-one is saying that you want your daughter to die, quite the contrary, but we must make sure no one has any reason to think the hospital condones euthanasia. Do either one of you have any questions? If not, I need for both of you to sign this hospital summary release form. LaDonna, look closely at the signature line, it says, 'LaDonna Kingsford aka LaDonna Anderson.' The lawyers said it was necessary to word it this way because someone might have construed that you and Matthew were already husband and wife. Rest assured no one thinks that there have been any improprieties. It's legal eagle stuff, they think they know what's what."

At first neither one of us knew how to respond; such a magnanimous gesture on part of the hospital, a gift I'm sure LaDonna appreciates. I told LaDonna she should be proud that the hospital administration valued her as an esteemed member of their nursing staff. All too seldom in life our good deeds go unnoticed, it's nice to every once in a while have someone give us a pat on the back saying 'job well done'.

A long time ago I learned to rely on the Word of the Lord and not my immediate set of circumstances, yet, the power of God still amazes me. I never would have believed that Abby would ever left the CCU/ICU, let alone return to the hospice, coma or no coma.

Our relationship with Aunt Cissy changed a long time ago from professional to personal, which required a special hug and kiss each time we met. Aunt Cissy insisted upon taking a personal interest with all of her patients and families, but in our case she extended herself far beyond what she was accustomed. Just as Abby looked upon her as a grandmother figure she as well looked to Abby as her own granddaughter.

Seeing Abby for the first time back in the hospice was as if, she had never been in the CCU/ICU. I tried to convince myself that she was only sleeping and that she would reawaken any minute. It's hard to look upon my daughter and realize that her heart had slowed down almost to a full stop; the cancer having taken its toll weakening her body to the point of placing her young life in jeopardy on several occasions. Just three months away from her thirteenth birthday, her life hasn't even begun yet; there are so many joys so many things she will not be able to experience. Day by day Abby showed little improvement, a slight twinge or involuntary muscle jerk, her whole being is being controlled by her autonomic nervous system without conscious control.

I hold her hand much tighter now than ever before knowing that at any moment she could slip away. I'm helpless and hurting as only a grieving father could feel. Abby's life was in the hands of God and the timeframe is his alone.

I keep looking for just a glimmer or twinkle of life in her eyes. I keep searching for reason and understanding, but find none.

LaDonna has decided that if she and I were to begin reading aloud to Abby maybe she would be drawn to the sound of our voice, rather than reaching to a bright light at the end of a dark tunnel. LaDonna also had another grand idea, what if we had on open Bible study just like we did before she became ill. I could read subject and verse, give explanation, ask her questions as if she were really awake. After all, what could it hurt? Recently I was reading in Psalms and came across the Lord's Prayer so I decided that *Psalms 23* would be a good topic to read to Abby. I asked LaDonna to read the scripture verbatim verse by verse, I would then follow-up by giving an all-inclusive explanation suitable for a young child's understanding.

LaDonna began by reading aloud, "The LORD is my shepherd; I shall not want."

I responded by saying, "Abby, this one is really a no-brainer; you already know from previous studies how God used the analogy of Christ as being the 'Good Shepard' and how he would provide and take care of us, 'His Flock'. By giving our lives to Christ allowing him to lead us we will never want for anything. I don't think I'll even ask if it makes any sense to you, which would only be insulting your intelligence and my ability to teach you even the basics."

"He maketh me to lie down in green pastures; he leadeth me beside the still waters; He restoreth my soul."

I responded by saying, "Sweetheart, I know you understand how important it is to take care of your pets and animals; to make sure they have food, water, clean cages or places to live in, right. When God is using the example of green pastures and still waters he is referring to our day-to-day living conditions. When I was a young boy just a little younger than you, during the summers we would go and visit my Uncle Herman who was a sheep and goat rancher, raising sheep and Angora goats for their wool. My Uncle Herman explained to me that he had to make sure his animals were only allowed to feed in green meadows or pastures because the ewes, pronounced 'U's', the mother sheep, needed rich nutritional grassland to feed on, in order to make sure they could produce enough milk they needed to feed their babies close to a clean slow-moving water supply. Uncle Herman also said that that it was extremely sad, but sheep and goats weren't the smartest animals God ever created, because sheep have been know to die of thirst standing right next to a water supply that perhaps was muddy or running too fast. I mean talk about being finicky and fussy, it's hard to believe that they were standing right next to water and still choose not to drink the water, but then again I guess the same is true for some people. By allowing Christ to be our shepherd he will bring spiritual peace and harmony to our often turbulent and hectic lives. Sweetie—I sure hope you're getting this, it's really important stuff. Abby, think back and try to remember what I explained to you concerning God's gift to mankind, his gift of 'free-will'. By accepting Jesus as our shepherd we must do so willingly by our own accord or choice. The most important decision by choice any person will ever make in their life is to accept Christ as their shepherd or choose to reject him standing right beside him."

"He leadeth me in the paths of righteousness for his name's sake."

I responded by saying, "Abby, this one I know you already understand. God has shown us that the only way to find everlasting peace through Christ our savior is by knowing what to do in the first place. How do we do that? By way of reading his revealed written word, the Bible. Remember when the disciples asked Jesus to teach them how to pray and he said that they should begin by saying, 'Our Father which art in Heaven...', it could only be found by reading what God had written in the Bible to learn how to pray correctly; well the same is true to develop righteousness, if we don't know what it is—how can we do it. Any answer that we may need can always be found by reading the Bible and by praying asking God for direction."

"Yea, though I walk through the valley of the shadow of death, I will fear no evil: for thou art with me; Thy rod and thy staff they comfort me."

I explained saying, "Because I am a child of God I no longer have anything to fear anything from evil because God has shown me the way, his rod will protect me, his staff will guide me and I have found comfort in the presence of the Lord."

"Thou preparest a table before me in the presence of mine enemies: thou anointest my head with oil; my cup runneth over. Surely goodness and mercy shall follow me all the days of my life: and I will dwell in the house of the LORD for ever."

I answered by saying, "Sweetheart, remember a few minutes ago we learned that any answer to any question could be found in the Bible, well in this verse we learn that God has prepared a way for us to receive his blessings even in the presence of sin. God has promised each of us everlasting life by anointing our souls originally with concentrated oil, however after Christ was put to death on the cross we were then concentrated by the blood of Christ for blessings we can't even begin to understand. God has given us a great deal more than what we actually need not only in this life but in our spiritual life to come. By accepting Jesus as our personal savior we are guaranteed his goodness and mercy for all time and eternity. Abby, like I told you before we can only speak for ourselves—as for me, I know I plan on serving the Lord my God for ever. Well sweetie—what do you think? What it really comes down to is how we choose to live our lives and by the choices that we each make that will ultimately determine our future and the spiritual journeys we will take. Some will choose to live their lives in a good and righteous manner; other's will choose to live a life against all of God's teachings. It's a matter of choice."

After LaDonna and I finished reading the Lord's Prayer we had hoped that somewhere along the way we would have seen some glimmer of hope, some movement, some sign that she understood that not only we were there with her in her room, but we were there sharing a message of God's eternal love with her.

"LaDonna, did you see what I saw,—was my mind playing tricks on me?" I asked, "Did she actually move her eye lids?"

LaDonna looked up at me and gestured by a nod of her head as if to say no. I realized that it was probably only wishful thinking on my part, but I had hoped.

"Matthew," LaDonna said, "I don't want to get your hopes up but a little voice deep-down inside me keeps telling me that if Abby continually hears your voice, her subconscious mind will try and resurface. Let's find something you can just read or perhaps tell her a story, but before you do, let's pray together and ask God for his help."

As much as I hated to admit it, I was still at a loss as to why Abby remained in a comatose state. The doctors have done their best to describe in lay-terms the reasons, yet despite their efforts I know little more now then I did seven days ago when she first went into heart failure.

"LaDonna, I need your help. Please help me understand why she doesn't wake-up, after-all her little body as gone through why this?" I asked.

"Sweetheart, I know how trying it is for you. I have seen your good days and I have seen your bad, I have come to know your strengths and I have even come to know that tender side you try your best to keep hidden. Matthew, I think over the last—what's it been, almost two years now since we first met down on the medical wing, anyway, in all this time I think I finally figured out when best to talk to you—as well as knowing, when you need to talk to me.

"Let me try and simplify where we are at this exact precise moment. Three days ago Abby's body just shut-down because her heart wasn't able to pump enough blood to sustain normal bodily functions for whatever the reasons. So to even make it simpler;

because she couldn't breathe correctly, her heart couldn't send enough oxygen to her brain, and although her heart never stopped beating she did stop breathing in a normal manner; to breathe in—to breathe out supplying her brain with the right amount of oxygen; because of imbalance of oxygen a metabolic disturbance took place in her brain function. Now, a metabolic coma is the result of anything that interferes with the functioning of the cerebral cortex. Any decrease in the delivery of oxygen, glucose sugars or sodium levels to the brain sends mixed signals to the good functioning parts of the brain, that when people simply just go into a deep sleep. Sweetheart is this making sense?"

I turned around to LaDonna and told her I was glad she was there with me. I was really trying to understand. I was fearful, but not afraid. Just as the night turned into day and we were greeted each morning by a new quandary of opportunity, I had always tried my best to have an open mind and accept what God gave me with a optimistic heart, which, I might add, at times could be rather difficult.

A few years ago a fund-raising campaign aimed at young Christian believers intended to promote 'thought before action' by outwardly proclaiming their faith by wearing interfaith jewelry designs from gold rings to rubber wrist-band imprinted with the letters *WWJD—What Would Jesus Do*. Sadly to say, the movement lasted but a short time despite the fact it was a brilliant idea. Using the same ideology I have asked myself WWJD, concerning my daughter's dreaded disease. The only answer I can find is to stand fast on faith unfettered.

Placing my faith in what I know to be true no matter how heavy the burden or how dark the moment may be, I believe God performs an infinite number of miracles each day from touching the heart of a drug abused non-believer to rescuing a young run-a-way girl off the streets from a life of prostitution; if it were not for his divine intervention I wonder how many more would be lost to a sacrilegious world wanting a quick-fix for everything including that of religion.

"LaDonna—I've got it. You wanted me to read out loud to Abby, well an idea just came to me, what if I you and I have an open discussion on the foundations of our beliefs?" I said.

"That's a great idea, Matthew," LaDonna responded, "how do we start? I've got it—why don't you start by telling me the history of how the Christian Bible came about. I'm sure you know a lot more about it than I do, actually Matthew I have always accepted it on face value but know very little about its beginning."

"Okay then, just follow my lead and jump in anywhere you feel comfortable with," I said, "let's pull a chair on both sides of Abby's bed that way we can kinda form a triangle between the three of us. "LaDonna, before we begin do you think that Abby has any understanding of what's going on around her? I mean do you think that's it's possible she can honestly hear what we've saying?" I asked.

"Matthew, I can't really say only God knows for sure. But I do think that the Holy Spirit will somehow guide our thoughts and love to Abby and she will have a 'knowing' someday," LaDonna said.

"LaDonna, now don't take this the wrong way," I said, "but sitting with Abby now is nothing more than a death-watch. She doesn't need us to feed her; she is fed by intravenous tubes. She doesn't require any assistance with her bladder or bowels; she has a catheter and wears diapers, you or one of the floor nurses see to that when she needs to be changed. Her airway has been removed, I mean Abby is just here, barely alive, as we know it. She doesn't require any help or assistance to lie there in her unconscious vegetative state. The nursing staff comes in every three or four hours to turn her to guard against ulceration's. All you and I do is sit here, watch and wait, for what is yet to come. I still keep asking myself over and over—why?"

"Darling, I wish I had an easy answer for you, but I don't. This is the one time that we have to allow and just accept whatever each day may bring," responded LaDonna.

We both just sat there in silence trying to regain a certain level of acceptance of the world we had been thrust into, a world which seemed totally out of control and out of our hands.

"Ya know girls, believing in the Bible has been the only sanctuary that makes any sense to me—believing that each line and precept was truly inspired by the hand of God," I said.

"Wait, wait, wait Matthew. I don't want it to seem as if I'm correcting you but as a teacher yourself you know the importance of using correct grammar and English whether or not Abby can hear what we might be saying or not, I still think it's important to...," LaDonna blurted out interrupting me in mid sentence.

"You're right, LaDonna," I said, "I shouldn't use words like 'ya know' or 'kinda'—I agree, it doesn't set a good example."

Chuckling to myself, I intended to explain how living with Abby I simply couldn't help myself picking-up some of her inappropriate slang's and habits, although perfectly normal for children of her age. Just as I was beginning to apologize LaDonna placed her forefinger of her right hand against her lips as if to say, 'don't say another word'; somehow through non-verbal communication I realized what she was doing, she only said what she did for Abby's benefit just in case she could hear what we were saying.

I went on to say, "Alright then ladies, I'll continue. The Bible is believed to be the 'revealed inspired word of God' with a timeline somewhat inconclusive and subject to conjecture but it has been adjudged based on archeological finds and known documents to have been written between the years of 1400 B.C. to around 175 A.D., at best guess theologians have speculated that some 40 different men wrote various parts of the Bible, but there has never been any concrete proof found.

"The writers were from all walks of life from simple fisherman and farmers to even a king from Jerusalem. One was a Roman tax collector, another one was a physician but the majority of the writers were merely men who God had touched with a message for their fellow man."

"Except for the first five books of the Old Testament, Genesis to Deuteronomy known as the 'Books of Moses' or the Hebrew Torah, the remaining 34 books of the Old Testament and the 29 books of the New Testament were all written by different authors spanning a period of time of some 1400 plus years.

"Matthew, can you tell me if there were any women writers in the holy Bible?" LaDonna asked.

"Sweetheart, I can…"

LaDonna interrupted me once again in mid-sentence, asking Abby with glee, "Did you hear your father? He called me sweetheart. Isn't that nice?"

"LaDonna, can I continue?" I asked as she blobbed her head up and down. "What I started to say is that I can only tell you that there are some books in the Old Testament that do not give the author's name. But remember what I said, it really doesn't matter whether any of the text was written by men or women. However, there has always been some conjecture as to whether or not the book of Ruth, a Moabite woman who converted to Judaism was revered in Jewish history as the Great-Grandmother of King David, and the book of Esther who although Jewish became the Queen of Persia, wrote their own respective letters.

"With the possible exception of the apostle writers it would have been highly unlikely that any of the other contributors could have known one another quite simply because of the timeline between various texts, in some cases several hundred years.

"Matthew, why do think you God thought it was necessary to have his words written down instead of just placing them in our hearts? LaDonna asked.

"Well first of all, I would even think about trying to second-guess what God had on his mind. LaDonna, I could tell you the Bible says this, or shows us that, and perhaps teaches us by examples on how to prepare ourselves for eternal life, but to keep it simple, I believe the Bible's primary purpose was and always has been to show mankind that the only way to achieve life-everlasting is through Jesus Christ our Savior. To answer the second part of your question; God doesn't want blind obedience that he could have mandated at creation, I believe he wants the respect and honor he deserves not under compulsion or restraint but by our openly accepting his love, compassion and generosity choosing to do so on our own accord by his gift of 'free-will'. If God embedded his words instinctively in our hearts we would no longer have free-will to choose one way or another on our own. Does that make sense to you now, LaDonna?"

"Besides from believing on faith that what we know as 'The Holy Bible' is true and correct it's important to remember that the word of God is not the book of bound pages itself but rather the meanings held upon those pages. The word of God is something mankind can't see or tangibly touch or feel, but we can perceive its spirit all around us if we are receptive to its very nature.

"LaDonna, for me the mere fact that a grouping of writings known as the Holy Bible is not just a book of mishmash-hodgepodge inconsistent theory; holding to reason or logic with conflicting story lines, letters and essays—but rather, a complete book of several interconnected messages written by different men over a period of a thousand years telling us a continuous story from beginning to end. This is more than enough evidence for me that it could only have been accomplished by the direct hand of God giving 'His Divine Inspiration' to each author separately without private interpretation."

"Matthew, I never heard a concise summary of the Bible before—it was really interesting," LaDonna said. "If truth be told, I can't believe how much I didn't know."

"LaDonna, do you think it did any good, I mean do you think maybe Abby understood what I was saying?" I asked.

"Sweetheart, I can't say for Abby, but for me I learned a great deal.

Within minutes Aunt Cissy poked her head in the door asking LaDonna if she could see her for a few minutes. Believing to be alone with Abby, I leaned over the head of her bed closed my eyes and in a faint whisper I prayed, "Lord, there's no way of knowing if our talking aloud is helping or not but just in case it is, I don't want to miss any opportunity that might bring Abby back to me, even for just a few minutes. I pray in the name of Jesus that somehow someway I'll have the opportunity to at least touch her heart and let her know once again how much I love her. And thank you for the love that LaDonna has given me."

LaDonna had returned to the room without my knowing and apparently overheard bits and pieces of my prayer.

"Matthew," she asked, "Can I share something with you?"

"I remember when my little brother died," she said, "It was during the summer months shortly after I graduated from high school, I was excited about making plans to attend nursing school in the fall, my brother Dale was having quite a hard time accepting that I would be living in the dorm away from home. He and I were very close almost inseparable; it seemed as if he always wanted to tag-along wherever I went, never having the heart to say 'no' his presence finally just became commonplace. Even though I was seven years older than Dale not having any other siblings I was the one who looked out for his well being most of the time. At first it was because of the hours our parents worked which quickly changed to a necessity as he grew older. Neither one of our parents ever seemed to ever have enough time to concern themselves to what we may want or need, don't get me wrong, they provided for life's essentials but little else.

"I made sure Dale had an afternoon snack right after school, saw to it that he finished his homework before my parents got home, and if we had any free-time after we had dinner and the kitchen was cleaned-up, I always washed—he always dried the dishes, then and only if all of our other chores were done, he and I would step out in the backyard to toss his baseball around for a little while.

"One day shortly after learning to ride his bicycle on his own without any assistance from me to help him find his balance, he had a mishap. I remember the incident very well; it was on a Saturday, both my parents were at home and Dale excitedly made up his mind he wanted to show Mom and Dad how well he was doing. They both declined saying they were busy with my mother speaking up telling him 'why not have LaDonna watch you—LaDonna go with your brother.' Before I could even slip on my shoes to go outside we heard a loud screeching cry, Dale had fallen off bicycle hitting his head on the concrete slab. No visible cuts or gashes just a few scrapes. Reluctantly, my mother took him to emergency room complaining all the way there while I held him in my arms, wiping away his tears, saying she just knew she was going to miss her bridge game. After a quick exam without any x-rays the doctor told Mother to take him home, once again my mother kept harping going on and on how she knew it wasn't anything in the first place, but a waste of time.

"That same evening after we had all gone to bed, Dale came to me crying saying his head hurt. I woke-up my parents and by the time they decided that maybe they should go back to the hospital, he fell unconscious and died the next morning from a cerebral aneurysm.

"Matthew, my parents rarely showed affection to anyone let alone to one another. They were good people in their own way, but didn't have a clue as to showing concern or compassion for anyone, they just didn't know how.

"My family was not atheists but not exactly religious believers either. Mother always had fresh clean clothes set out on Saturday evenings for us to wear to Sunday school, a glass of orange juice was poured and wrapped with plastic wrap sitting in the refrigerator generally next to a muffin or sweet roll of some kind; mother didn't want us to make a mess trying to fix our own breakfast, we were to be quiet on Sunday mornings so she could sleep in. It was Dad who would grab a cup of coffee the Sunday morning newspaper from the driveway as we went out the door, he would drive us to a Lutheran Church just a few blocks away from our house and sit in the car reading his newspaper waiting for Dale and I to come out after Sunday school. I honestly believe it afforded him time away from mother because he never seemed to mind taking us each week.

"My brother and I knew our parents loved us, but not once can I recall them saying anything remotely connected to 'I love you'.

"Matthew, right after my brother's funeral the house was full of family, friends, and neighbors. My mother came and sat down next to me placing her arm around over my shoulders and said, 'I don't pretend to know why God does what he does. Your grandmother always said that she was only certain of two things in life; the first being that she knew from the bottom of her heart that the angels in heaven cried for the very first time when Jesus was crucified, and the second thing she knew as sure as the sun came up each morning was that the angels also cry every time a child dies.'

"Sweetheart, I'm only telling you about my family life as a young girl because I think it's something you needed to hear; you're not the only one who has ever endured agonizing emotional pain and distress. Once I started nursing school I never looked back and believe me I have no regrets. I made myself a promise a long time ago, that if I were lucky enough, fortunate enough and privileged enough to somehow find that one special someone and we had children I would never allow either my husband or my children to go wanting for the simple things in life, the kind gestures, moments of spending quality time and most importantly telling them each and every day that they are loved beyond words.

"Matthew, I want you to know that I empathize and appreciate what you're feeling having been there myself. When it pains you to look back, and you're frightened to look ahead, look directly beside you—I'll be there.

"My Darling; love begins in so many ways—but true love always ends with a tear; a tear of joyous memories of a full life together, a solitary tear for remembrance of adoration, benevolence and caring. Tears of true love can't help but be carried to the grave when a loved one departs; for love never ceases—it is the only treasure you can take with you."

I sat there and thought over LaDonna's remarks; she was right, I have forgotten that there are those who have even experienced greater lose than mine. Her sharing gave me new insight of what I have been feeling; it also showed me how capable she was of being hurt or wounded.

I'm tired, so very tired; more so mentally than physically. Exhausted, drained and weary are all part of my everyday vocabulary. I know LaDonna has to be as exhausted and played out as I am. I finally convinced her to go to her apartment, telling her to have a long bath and refresh herself. She was somewhat hesitant at first but I persuaded her that she needed to. It wasn't until I promised that I would do the same that she finally agreed.

Even in the face of death, life for the living continues. Abby could linger for a long time; Dr. J has indicated that only God knows her appointed time, as for me—I will cherish whatever time table I have. I have put my own life on hold just to be near Abby having no regrets and shall continue to do so for as long as it takes.

Aunt Cissy tried to tell me months ago that it was imperative that I take care of myself, Dr. J prescribed vitamins lecturing what good would I be to Abby if I became ill. I haven't said anything to anyone not even LaDonna, but I fear Aunt Cissy might be right. I haven't felt well for a few weeks now, just out-of-sorts in a physical way. I can only guess that it's probably stress related reinforced by the lack of a good nights sleep.

I haven't been home for a several weeks now—there are so many things I need to do; stop by the post office, balance my checkbook, and pay a few bills, catch-up on my correspondence. I knew that somehow I need to make the time to take care of some personal business but never found the time.

LaDonna has given so much—sacrificing her own life all under the auspices of love; I believe although not fully certain, initially it was her care and concern for Abby just wanting to be of help to a single father trying his best to raise a child all alone, who had become ill.

For some strange reason single women seem to gravitate to single fathers raising children on their own, for the most part single fathers tend to be disoriented in so many different areas. One of the many advantages of going to parochial school was the non-academic training the priests were so famous for. There was one priest who stood out among the rest; his name was 'Father Walsh' an Irish priest who immigrated here to the states early in the nineteen-twenties. He spoke with a heavy Irish dialect a brogue not unlike Father O'Malley in "Going My Way." He was just a little wisp of a man standing well under five feet who carried a big-stick literally. He was famous for his statement to each class he taught saying, "Gentlemen, if any of you hooligans are ever fortunate enough to finds wives who might be in the hospital bearing your child, each of you must know how to survive domestically—if I teach you nothing else before you leave my classroom you will know how to sew on a button, how to hand-wash a pair of socks and know which knobs and buttons turn on the stove to heat-up a can of soup—how you open the can will be up to each of you!"

Even as a man I soon developed a maternal instinct in which to raise Abby. Luckily, there were books written on the subject.

I told LaDonna before she left that I didn't want to see her until the next noon, she too needed time away to properly bathe, if nothing else just lay and soak in the tub. Here at the hospital grabbing a shower hasn't been a problem, but I am well familiar with the need especially for women wanting to take a bubble bath, or at least I recall that's how Abigail felt.

LaDonna has not only given to Abby but to me as well. Now, she needs to give to herself. Knowing LaDonna, she won't listen; if I were a betting man I would bet she won't be gone but just a few hours before she returns. It was just as I had thought, LaDonna returned not six hours later. She said she had plenty of time to do what she wanted and even stopped by Geno's Italiano Restaurante and brought-in something to eat that wasn't made in the hospital cafeteria.

"I decided that since we can't go out and have a nice meal, I would bring one in," LaDonna said. "I hope you like Italian. I didn't know if you liked red or white sauces, so I bought both, a nice red burgundy marinara and classic Alfredo sauce. Here—smell this garlic bread."

"LaDonna," I said, "you really shouldn't have. You should have stayed home and gotten a good night's rest. Look, I'm selfish, in one way I'm glad you didn't because I must admit that I missed your not being here and I appreciate the gesture of bringing food in. The food downstairs isn't all that bad, but it is awfully bland. There isn't a hot dish downstairs that the cafeteria cooks make, that I haven't tried at least once, and believe me—once was plenty in some cases. Anyway, let's get back to your needing some rest, LaDonna you must somehow someway if for no other reason to pacify me, please."

LaDonna stood there with a sheepish grin as if to say, *Whatever you say, Matthew.*

"Here, sit and eat while it's still hot," she said, "I also picked up a quart of Italian spinach. It's fresh. Do you like Italian spinach?"

"LaDonna, I like most any vegetable," I responded.

There was so much that LaDonna and I didn't know about one another. We didn't have the opportunity to learn and grow as most couple would do, not having a typical get-acquainted courtship. We met, and we met and fell in love without the wine and roses. It was only through general conversations that we were able to ascertain bits and pieces of information such as, which would you like green beans or spinach tonight, the spaghetti or meatloaf, oh—I just love that color. LaDonna and I were living in the moment and gave no thought of exchanging informational likes and dislikes.

It's absolutely delightful to have someone think about you, to care about you, to make a fuss over you. It's nothing less than heavenly.

The meal was truly enjoyable. Having finished, LaDonna looked to me and said that it was my turn to go home and if I didn't want an argument I should just pick myself up and head out the door assuring me that all would be just fine. She suggested that I go home take a long shower and get a good night's sleep not to return until the morning. "Matthew, isn't that a novel idea—to sleep in a bed for a change, especially your very own bed," she said. "You'll enjoy it. Besides when was the last time you gave yourself permission to think of yourself for a change? Another thing, my father use to tell Dale and I, and I quote, 'don't do as I do—do as I say do.' Get my drift?"

I took LaDonna up on her offer and went home. Mrs. Bishop, our friendly next door neighbor, who in many ways resembled Aunt Bea from Mayberry, came running over the minute she saw my car pull into the drive. "Matthew," she said, "How's little Abby?" she asked. I explained everything the best that I could as we stood on the front porch.

Mrs. Bishop was a widow late in her seventies whose husband died many years earlier; she always had a tendency to look-in after Abby and me. She was always bringing over some sort of casserole or a pan of baked goods right from her oven. She had no other family and somewhat adopted us as her own. She didn't get around very well having arthritis in both knees and feet, but she managed. Before Abby's illness we always checked with her before going grocery shopping to see if she needed anything. She had a need to give and I was grateful for her love and friendship.

I gave her a key to the house when I first took Abby to the hospital just in case she needed one. She would hobble over each day sometimes using her cane sometimes not, to check on things and feed Abby's dog. During this past year what few times I did come home, she always met me before I had a chance to get my key in the front door. Every few days I would call from the hospital just to check-in with her; throughout his past year before even before our coming to the hospice every Wednesday afternoon without fail she would call and talk to Abby, later telling me how she missed their telephone conversations after the coma.

It seemed foreign walking in the front door, as if I had gone into a stranger's home. Mrs. Bishop, that kind dear lady, kept the house cleaned and dusted. I asked her not to, but she did nonetheless. I think she somehow managed to talk her cribbage group, all ladies about her own age to lend a helping hand before she would play with them. Generally she liked entertaining her friends in the enclosed garden room of my home; supposedly to keep Deeohgee company, then again, Mrs. Bishop would go on to say it was so beautifully decorate with the white wicker furniture and Mexican style tile with all the amenities anyone would ever want. When I had it constructed I had a wet-bar built with a mirrored back splash, a half-size refrigerator and wrap around countertops. Whenever they left that little refrigerator was always well stocked from chicken salad to homemade cheese balls.

I had walked throughout the house looking into each room. The house itself seemed so big and empty. I stepped into Abby's room and I just couldn't contain my tears. My mind ran back to the hospital where she lay motionlessly. I remembered sitting on the floor in this very room so long ago, crying then, as I am now.

Without thought, I found myself walking up the steps to the attic. It has been a long time since I spoke with Abigail. Opening the attic door I noticed the room was musty and stale with a faint odor of moisture. I sat down in my usual seat upon the settee. I didn't see any reason to change old habits. I talked to Abigail as I always had, telling her anything and everything. But this time I included the details concerning LaDonna. Having spent the better part of an hour just talking aloud to Abigail, as I stood up to leave I noticed a faint smell or odor of roses. *Strange*, I thought to myself—memories playing tricks on the subconscious. I left the attic, going downstairs with the idea of showering and taking a brief nap.

Just as I was drying-off, the doorbell rang. I grabbed my bath robe and proceeded to the front door. I opened the door and found Mrs. Bishop holding a plate of pasta, which she said she had just prepared for me. She said she didn't want to keep me, but knew that I didn't have anything in the house to eat. She also said that she hadn't fed "Deeohgee", but would come back if I wanted her to. She chuckled and remarked how funny the dog's name was. "You know Matthew; every time I think of the name that Abby gave that dog I can't help but think how cute it is. Only Abby could think-up the name by spelling it—who else ever would have thought of D*O*G," she said. I thanked Mrs. Bishop for the pasta and told her I would feed Abby's dog before leaving. It was a beautiful gesture, her bringing over the pasta. Because I had just eaten with LaDonna I didn't have the heart to say anything. I was full and definitely not hungry, especially for pasta. I knew that Mrs. Bishop would have her feeling's hurt if she thought I didn't eat it; so I decided to transfer it to some plastic freezer containers placing it in the large freezer out in the garage. I washed her plate and sat in on the kitchen counter where she would notice it the next time she was over.

Before taking my shower, I had already removed the comforter from my bed, pulling back the blanket and top sheet, surprisingly but I noticed the sheets were fresh, making a mental note to thank Mrs. Bishop. I didn't want to waste any time, just as LaDonna said, I needed a good night's sleep in my own bed, and I was looking forward to it.

I knelt down and said my prayer's in the privacy of my own bedroom. It felt good. Before I fell asleep, I started to call the hospital to check-in with LaDonna, and then decided against it thinking that she might be sleeping herself. I crawled into bed and the next thing I knew it was morning—I had slept the entire night without hearing a sound. Upon awaking, I dressed and returned to the hospital.

On the drive back to the hospital I stopped off at a little donut shop over on Seventh Street, Clause's Donuts, as I recalled they made the best glazed donuts ever. LaDonna was kind enough to think of bringing dinner the night before; the least I could do was bring her a jelly-filled donut.

When I reached the hospice, LaDonna was walking out of the nurse's lounge. She had been relieved long enough to freshen-up by the charge nurse. Seeing LaDonna with her hair slightly damp, I felt somewhat ashamed that it was I who had a good night's sleep knowing she probably slept in my recliner. The recliner isn't bad for a quick snooze, but it wasn't intended to actually sleep in. I came to the realization then and there that LaDonna and I needed to rotate our sleeping schedules. Before LaDonna came along, the recliner wasn't all that bad for me. However, I can't allow her to sleep in that chair night after night, as I have done.

"Hi there," she said, as she gave me a quick kiss on the cheek as I walked into Abby's room.

"Did you sleep well? Was I right? Didn't it feel good to go home and get a good night's sleep?" she asked.

"First of all, anything new with Abby? Now to answer your question," I said, "Sweetheart, do you recall our talking the other day about Psalm 23 where it says, 'He maketh me to lie down in green pastures; He leadeth me beside the still waters; He restoreth my soul.' Well, that's what it was like. My bed was the serenity of lying in the green pasture, I felt renewed as if actually sitting beside a pool of still water, and talk about feeling rejuvenated—God really did restore my soul. Thank you darling; although the reprieve was great I felt a great lost not having you near. If truth be known, I have grown so accustomed to your presence, I'm lost without you.

LaDonna placed her arms around my neck giving me a kiss unlike ever before, a kiss of love and passion, a kiss that only a husband and wife would appreciate.

Without saying another word LaDonna and I sat there next to Abby's bed and ate our donuts. "Funny," I said, looking in Abby's direction, "Abby loves jelly-filled donuts, too, just like you."

# Chapter 11: Thy Kingdom Come— Elysian Fields

"Sweetheart," LaDonna said, "there's no easy way to ask, but I need to know if you have made arrangements for funeral services yet. I would also like your help in understanding more about funeral rites, I've never buried anyone before and I really don't know what to expect or what's expected of me standing in for Abby's mother. I'm so glad you understand the Bible, but what does it say about God's expectations from us—do you know?"

"LaDonna, if you look in my briefcase you'll find a folder with all of the information; take a look at it when you feel up to it, it might answer some other questions I'm sure you'll have somewhere along the way. Being Jewish by birthright I tried to accommodate and maintain respect for both the Jewish and Christian doctrines of eternal rest. I have never considered my Jewish roots as being a religion—a way of life yes, but not a religious belief. Darling I don't know if I have all the answers and what little I do know I've read either in the Bible or the Torah. Yet, there are still a few things I have never been able to sort out in my mind," I answered.

"Matthew, what do you mean when you say Jewish birthright— do Jewish people have different burial practices then we do?" LaDonna asked.

"If you meant Christian practices when you referred to the 'we do' then the answer is yes, there are a great many differences based upon teachings found in both the Jewish and Christian doctrines.

"First of all, LaDonna, do you remember when I explained to you that in Judaism, family bloodlines are matriarchal with lineage traced through the female line. In ancient rabbinical tradition a person has to be born of a Jewish mother in order to be Jewish. According to tradition, the Jewish nation is inherited through the mother while their tribe is inherited through the father. This has always been the case, you may not obviously know who a child's father is but with full certainty you always know who the mother is. Today the only standard that must be met is that only one of the parents must be born Jewish; my mother an orthodox Jew gave birth to me making me Jewish hence Abby is considered Jewish by biological heredity.

"Just as there is a Jewish way of life there is also a Jewish way of death. According to Jewish interpretation of the Old Testament Law, burial had to occur within 24 hours of the very same day, however this is not the case today, it is still preferred out of tradition but not mandated. Originally, its primary concern was because the body was considered to be ceremonially unclean and therefore had to be prepared for burial as soon as possible. Traditional Judaism argues against embalming the body for several reasons; embalming was considered an act of mutilation of the body which is by itself an act of irreverence, another reason why embalming was forbidden was the sanctity of the blood. Jewish law was very strict concerning respect and reverence of a dead body.

"As believers in the gospels and having accepted Christ as our savior, I believe Jesus set the example for mankind to follow in all things—including the death process. When Jesus was taken from the cross his body was handed over for burial preparation. His body was washed, anointed with various oils and spices, and wrapped with special, grave-clothes of white linen that contained spices which are mentioned in John 19: 39-40. His body after preparation was placed in a 'tomb' belonging to a rich Jewish man named Joseph of Arimathea, honed out of solid rock. LaDonna, this is one of the areas I am having problems with. Jesus's body wasn't embalmed, he wasn't cremated and he wasn't dressed in the finest clothing like we do today.

"I realize the reason why traditional Jews were buried in a simple white garment known as a shroud made without any pockets; it signified no distinction that all men were equal rich or poor alike in the eyes of God, the concept of not having any pockets in the burial clothes symbolized that none of man's material possessions can be taken with him after death.

"Darling, is all of this making sense to you?" I asked.

"Please don't stop, it really interesting. But I have a question; what about the use of flower arrangements during the funeral?" LaDonna asked.

"Although depictions of flowers used at funerals are found in the Talmud, if you remember I told you that the Talmud is a sacred-text of rabbinic discussions on everything from Jewish law, ethics and customs and believe me it also covers anything and everything you can think of in-between, anyway, most Orthodox rabbis discourage the use any floral decorations at the funeral or on the casket on the belief that the money spent on such ornate appearance is actually wasted, money should be used and spent on the living.

"Two other things come to mind I need to share with you; the coffin is never opened for viewing during the service and photographs are discouraged. It has always been held that as Jews we should hold a mental image of the deceased etched in our hearts and minds as they were at their finest. Jewish mourning is quite different than that found in Christianity. Mourning varies based upon the faction, but generally modern Orthodox Jewish tradition believes mourning lasts seven days, most of the other Jewish sects believe three days mourning is sufficient.

"Matthew, what do you mean other Jewish sects—Jewish is Jewish, isn't it?" LaDonna asked.

"Well, not exactly, darling," I said. "Just as we see vast differences and beliefs between variously other religions, the Catholics believe this, the Methodist believe that, the Baptist believe still yet another doctrine, the Jewish people are not any different either—each faction holding to what I like to refer to as a 'cafeteria affinity', having something for everybody of which to pick and choose. This is yet another area of concern for me. Sweetheart—I can't help but believe that no matter what, we have no right to establish doctrine on the basis of what we *hope* may be true, we must draw our knowledge from what the Bible *reveals* to be true!

"*Reconstructionists Jews* believe that Judaism is an evolving religion much more liberal than Reform Judaism—they do observe some Jewish Law if they choose to, not because it is a binding Law from God, but because of what they deem valuable cultural tradition."

"There you go with that 'Traditional' value system again," LaDonna said.

"I know, LaDonna, so much of this is rather odd and strange to someone who hasn't had a Jewish background, but none-the-less is fact," I said, continuing on to say, "*'Reform Judaism'* believes that the Torah was written by different human sources, rather than by God, and then later combined in books or volumes. While Reform Judaism does not accept the binding nature of 'halakhah' or Jewish Law, the Reformed movement does retain much of the values and ethics of Judaism as well as some of the practices. *'Conservative Judaism'* maintains that the ideas in the Torah come from God, but were transmitted by humans and contain a human component of possible error in translation. Conservative Judaism generally accepts the binding nature of the halakhah, but believes that the Law should adapt, absorbing aspects of the predominant culture while remaining true to Judaism's values. *Orthodox Jews* believe that God gave Moses the whole Torah, both the written and oral, at Mount Sinai. The 'Written Torah' refers to the first five books of the Bible; the 'Oral Torah' interprets and explains the Written Torah by rabbinical authority. Orthodox Jews believe that the Torah contains 613 'mitzvot' or commandments that are binding upon Jews. Modern Orthodox Jews strictly observe halakhah, but still integrate into modern society. The *Ultra-Orthodox Jews*, which includes Chasidic Jews, are very strict observing all mitzvot and do not integrate into modern society by dressing characteristically distinctive and living separately wearing the same black hat, the same velvet skullcap, the same dark wool jacket and pants and white business shirt with their untrimmed beards and long curled sidelocks of hair. Their beliefs stems back to biblical edicts found in Leviticus warning not to follow the idolatrous ways and customs of the pagans.

"There are a few things I have done concerning Abby's arrangements that you may not understand, so I better explain them. There is a very old traditional dating back thousands of years being buried in the hallowed ground of *Eretz Yisrael* 'the land of Israel', for those Jews not able to be buried there, a bit of earth from the land of Israel can be placed in the coffin. A few years ago long before Abby became ill I purchased an earthen jar made of baked clay from the holy land filled with the hallowed ground to be used in my coffin as well as Abby's, showing my respect for the beliefs of my mother and her matriarchal line. I also pre-arranged for coffins for both she and I made of simple pine where I had holes drilled in the bottom giving significance to the scripture saying 'Unto dust thou shall return' in Genesis 3:19. Now some things have changed—namely our getting married. Once we are married I would like it if you would agree to allow the same. I have also been thinking of something else I need to share with you. If you have no objections I would like to purchase a private family mausoleum where Abby, you and I can be interred."

"But, Matthew, I thought you told me that Jewish tradition forbid burial in mausoleums because of not being in contact with the ground," asked LaDonna, "but I don't care if…whatever you decide will be fine with me. All I know is that I love you and whatever happens to our physical bodies after our deaths are no big concern considering that since God is spirit, and we each return to him we must do so in spirit form as well and doesn't our earthly bodies just return to dust anyway? In any event, didn't you tell me that we are promised new bodies, bodies of spirit form?"

"Wow, either you have much more insight than I have understood you had or you were just given discernment by the Holy Spirit. Your right about typical Jewish tradition and the use of mausoleums; the Reformed movement is the only sect that allows the use of mausoleums, personally I'm beginning to wonder if it's wrong considering it's economic, environmental and ecological reasons in this day and age. They are always clean and dry unaffected by seasonal problems that delay burials such as frozen soil or frost on the ground, the muddy spring thaws makes it at times quite difficult to facilitate burial below ground. I'm not trying to find a way to circumvent doctrine or dogma, just giving myself another venue for interment.

"I keep thinking back to the illustration of Christ being buried in a tomb, a sepulture. I can't help but question like I said before that since he was our example why wasn't he buried below ground.

"LaDonna, there's more. Although I have not spoken with the memorial park for some time now I can see no reason that since personal family mausoleums are custom built why it wouldn't be possible to have it constructed without a floor and if that wouldn't fly for some reason, there may be some health department regulation I'm not aware of, none-the-less then have a layer of soil sandwiched between the casket and a concrete floor ensuring the concept of 'to dust you shall return'."

"LaDonna, I'm sure you figured it out by now, that Jewish tradition favors modesty and simplicity in its treatment of the dead. It's not that Jewish people are cheap and won't spend the money for a more elaborate funeral, it's because it is tradition.

"Darling, if you ever have the chance to see *Topol* who plays *Tevye*, the father of four daughters living in Russia under the rule of the czar, in *Fiddler on the Roof.* It is well worth the three hours of your time; not only entertaining but enlightening about Jewish culture. The whole play used symbolic reference to display meaning of traditions embedded in the hearts and minds of the Jewish people during times of hardship, explaining that if for no other reason everything in life is done for—*TRADITION.* When Tevye was asked why something was always done a certain way he always responded by saying any responding, 'You ask…how this tradition gets started?' I'll tell you—I don't know! But it's a tradition…and because of our traditions…every one of us knows who he is and what God expects him to do.'

"Darling, I'm not trying to disregard tradition; I only want to do what is best for my family, for you and Abby. So since you haven't any objections I will contact Memorial Gardens and see what I can arrange."

"Matthew, I want to change the subject for a moment; I have another question that isn't so unpleasant to think about. I know I'm the one who brought the subject up over burial arrangements, but I need a little reprieve from thinking about what I would rather not think about in the first place if you know what I mean," said LaDonna. "I'm been thinking about Abby's dreams, trying to find understanding especially where angels are concerned—is there some special way of identifying angelic contacts, I mean, how can anyone tell the difference between the good angels, bad or evil ones?"

Thinking for a minute I tried to recall information I had found and from what source to answer LaDonna's question. I began by saying, "Sweetheart, I don't have all the answers I wish I did. I have spent my entire life trying to find answers to questions I've considered important but there are still times I feel totally lost and haven't a clue.

"I think in order to identify good or evil anything, we each need a set of moral values beyond reproach and a good definition of exactly what 'good' is verses what exactly 'bad' is. How do we describe good; is it something that displays moral excellence or a distinguishing quality that may be admirable. Is it having desirable or positive qualities or perhaps something that's promotes or enhances our own well-being. I mean good is just good based on the context of facts or circumstances that surround a situation or event. At first thought one would automatically think that the opposite of good should be bad but not necessarily evil. 'Bad' has an expectation of being below standard, having negative or undesirable qualities of something. 'Evil' can be described as having a perverted—morally objectionable behavior, generally associated with deviant behavior departing substantially from the normal accepted practices within a given society, also the notion of evil holds a sinister diabolical demonic or satanic influence."

LaDonna sat there for a moment lost in thought and then asked, "Matthew—your explanation on just the good and bad seems somewhat long, is it really necessary to give that much consideration in describing good and evil?".

"LaDonna, that's the problem with most people, they tend to look for simple easy ways to understand what the scriptures may be telling them," I answered—adding, "Your question is not all that simple to understand. Let's leave out the concept of bad and concentrate of good verse evil, that way we can determine a relationship whether the difference between good and evil is absolute or relative. Any trait that is 'absolute' does not depends on anything else and is beyond human control without restriction, conditions or limitations. 'Relative' characteristics have no absolutes and only have significance in relation to something else.

"LaDonna, recalling back to the children Bible stories we heard as youngsters, originally all the angels were good angels. Lucifer started out as a good angel who worshiped God but because of his 'pride & greed' he rebelled against God and was expelled from heaven. As a result of that rebellion, he fell into disobedience and infinite number of angels numbering into the tens of thousands, fell with him, perhaps as many as one-third of all of the angelic multitude as indicated by reading Revelation 12. At any rate, he has a multitude of helpers known as demons to do his bidding. The Bible tells us clearly that the fallen angels have no redemption, simply because Christ did not atone for their sins.

"I'm like you, LaDonna; I, too, have been thinking about Abby's encounter and thank God that her dreams and visions were with angels of light.

"Satan is presented in the Bible as having a keen intellect; although at one time he stood in God's presence, he chose his own path and he knows with full certainty his ultimate consequence along with that of his demons will be an eternal existence in that infernal region known as hell. Now, is 'Hell' a place or a state of mind; ask a dozen different people and you'll get a dozen different answers. All I can tell you is that in 'Hell'—there will be the absence of the Holy Trinity. Can you even imagine living for all time and eternity in a void of the presence of our Lord and Savior and his Holy Spirit? I can't!"

"Matthew, how is it possible to identify the good angels from the bad ones?" LaDonna asked.

"Darling," I answered, "The Apostle Paul said there were many similarities between the two angels. When Jesus was on earth, Satan mustered all of his powers to try to persuade the Son of God from his calling. He tried to kill the Christ Child when Herod slaughtered the children less than two years of age in all the land around Bethlehem. When his plan failed, he tried to tempt Christ in the desert; time after time Satan tried to defeat Jesus, and was unsuccessful, of course. Christ said, "Now judgment is upon this world; now the ruler of this world will be cast out" as we read in John 12:31.

"The fear that Paul had for the saints in Corinth,"

"Matthew, let me stop you for a minute. Where is Corinth?" LaDonna asked.

"Corinth sometimes referred to as Korinthos, was an ancient city in Greece. It was a thriving urban center for its day only second of size to Athens, somehow from everything that I have read I always perceived that Paul had a special kinship to the people of Corinth quite possibly because they were ready to receive the gospel," I replied, continuing on to say, "Paul was afraid that 'the serpent who deceived Eve by his craftiness, might be able to lead the Corinthians astray from the simplicity and purity of their devotion to Christ', as he wrote in 2 Corinthians 11:3.

"LaDonna, not every miracle is from God; I wish it weren't so but even evil angels can and will do marvelous acts under the pretense of God with intention to deceive mankind from the truth of the Gospel of Christ. In 2 Thessalonians 2:9, we are warned to guard against false teachings of Satan telling us that he will come with 'all his power, signs and false wonders' to deceive.

"Good angels stand in God's presence seeing God as he actually is; the word 'angel' is a Greek word 'angelos', meaning "messenger—and they can only come when God sends them and only when they have a message to deliver or perform a specific function designated by God. The Bible is filled with references to angels, the Old and New Testament alike. Gabriel appearance to the

Virgin Mary is probably one of my favorite examples, then again when God led Israel out of Egypt, he sent his angel to do it. When Christ was tempted by Satan and needed to recuperate, angels appeared to him giving him strength. There are several hundred other references in the Bible concerning angels, always appearing as messengers with words of wisdom never detracting from the glory of God.

"Sweetheart, lets read Isaiah 6:3 together…here Isaiah draws a depiction of angels singing saying 'Holy, Holy, Holy is the Lord of hosts; the whole earth is full of His glory'! While we have the Bible out let also read in Revelation 5:11-12 where John describes what he saw in heaven, 'Then I looked, and I heard the voice of many angels around the throne and the living creatures and the elders; and the number of them was myriad's of myriads, and thousands of thousands, saying with a loud voice—Worthy is the Lamb that was slain to receive power and riches and wisdom and might and honor and glory and blessing.' "

"LaDonna—I do believe in angels and I know that you do as well. Aunt Cissy's research and documented study with her patients give credence to their existence. I also believe that they move in and out among us. How do we know we are being visited by angels of light and not darkness; darling, I wish I could give you a more concrete answer but I can tell you this, good angels have messages for those who are to receive the salvation of the Lord and bad angels will always try and convince you or tempt you to sin in some manner as we read in 1 Peter 5:8, Matthew 10:1 and Ephesians 6:11.

"Sweetheart, at first glace we may not always be able determine the good angels from the bad, but standing firm to our convictions on faith and telling them in the name of Jesus Christ to depart—they will.

"Matthew, my dear—I hate to say it, but I've been brain-dead my entire adult life I suppose, having just accepted on face value what others have told me concerning the gospels. I've never taken the time, actually I should say, I've never made the time to learn for myself what exactly the scriptures are and what they tell us. How did you ever manage the time raising a daughter, work and outside activities to read and learn from the scriptures?" LaDonna said, "It's astounding, your knowledge of angels. Is everything that you told me written down in the Bible?"

"Pretty much—yes, as a matter of fact some time ago at a Christian interfaith conference, I walked away with my head spinning with so much information I never realized existed before. I signed-up for this particular workshop entitled 'The Angels Among Us', and I had never been the same since. I have had two close encounters with angelic beings, the first I've shared with you when Abigail and I went skiing when we were in college and the second time I seldom talk about, I do think about it occasionally, without fail always on June 10th. It was twenty-six years ago and I can remember it as if it were yesterday."

"Matthew—whatever your reasons I'll believe what you say, honest I will. I know it can't be over something you may have done, you're the most honest person I've ever known!" LaDonna said.

"Sweetheart, it's neither. But the experience was so over-whelming almost so unbelievable I questioned my own sanity for a long time not wanting to accept the obvious.

"Like I said, it happened on June 10th a Friday night, I was young in my early twenties volunteering as a reservist with the police department here in Happy Valley."

"Matthew—you were a police officer, you never mention that before," LaDonna said.

"It was a long time ago before I started teaching. I had already graduated, had my teaching certification but at that point I was hired-on with the district yet. I had these ostentatious ideas of grandeur of being needed and wanting to save the world as most newly young college graduates do. I also knew that the board of education would see my community service as a plus when considering my application for a full-time teaching position. I have envisions of helping some young thug turn his life around becoming a productive member of society, but it wasn't at all that I expected. It wasn't at all like the cop's and robber's we see on television but more mundane;

the clerical side of taking reports and record keeping, directing traffic at the scene of an accident or when a traffic signal suddenly goes awry, answering telephones and taking messages for the regular officers when out on calls away from the station. Anyway, at the time I felt it was a good way to give something back to the community without much of a commitment. As reserve police officers we were allowed to ride with the regular officers and assist where needed without the added burden on the city to fund additional personnel. I was assigned to work the third shift, a midnight to 8:00 A.M. watch, Officer Morris and I were patrolling in the northeast section of the city when we received a call to respond to a '211' in progress..."

"Matthew—what's a 211?" LaDonna asked.

"Honey, a 211 is police jargon for armed robbery in progress. I wasn't concerned because I was with a regular officer who had years of experience, I was only there acting as his backup if necessary, he would handle all the dangerous stuff at least that's what I led myself to believe. Now LaDonna, as reservist we went to the same police academy and received the same training that the regular officers did, we were sworn-in with full arresting powers as were the regular full-time commissioned officers. We were not authorized to carry our side-arms when not in uniform and working as an adjunct, other than that we were police officer's sword to protect and serve. One of the main advantages of any city having a reserve command is that in case of crisis or emergency a ready-made trained division stands ready.

"I didn't even have the time to think if I were even afraid, because everything escalated so fast. When we arrived on the scene we witnessed one suspect holding a weapon exiting the front entrance of an all-night convenience store running around the corner to the back of the building, Officer Morris removed his weapon from his holster and gave chase as I went to the front door yelling-in to the clerk asking how many suspects and was anybody hurt—the clerk held up two fingers and shook his head side-to-side giving indication that no one was injured. I knew our backup was mere minutes away—it was standard operating procedure that two patrol units would be dispatched for any incident involving the use of weapons or violence, and immediately followed around the building to locate my partner when I heard a gunshot—my adrenalin was pumping fast and furious, I gave little thought for what I might find—looking directly in my path into the shadows I saw a figure of a man hunched-over some wooden crates, it was Officer Morris, my partner, he had been shot in the stomach, blood spurting rhythmically gushing to the cadence of his rapid heartbeat. There was no doubt the suspects were armed and dangerous. I knelt by his side placing my hands against the spurting wound applying pressure to slow down his bleeding, his bleeding was so perfuse I knew I wouldn't be able to stop it all together, he needed to be transported 'ASAP' to the medical center. I looked up and saw the outline of a dimly-lit silhouette of someone running in the far distance, I had no choice—helping my partner was my immediate concern, wondering to myself what happened to the second suspect, where could he have gone.

"Within seconds I heard a faint dissonant sound and felt as if someone had walked-up behind me. I twisted the trunk of body to over-look my right shoulder my hands still in place on Morris' wound, frozen with fear I saw a man holding a gun not three inches away from the back of my skull. I was stunned—fully conscious but frozen with fear unable to even speak. I stared at the barrel of that gun out of the corner of my eye, not quite able to believe what had just happened. Morris was gargling in his own blood as he tried to speak; he was really in a bad shape. 'Don't turn around' I heard a voice say, 'we didn't mean it—it just happened'. At that moment Morris reached up and grabbed me with one of his hands pulling me down to chest telling me in a barely audible whisper that his wound was an accident saying he shot himself as he stumbled over some vegetables crates in the dark.

"Anderson," Morris cried in a feeble utter "Pray for me, please."

"At that precise moment the young man dropped his gun to the ground and fell to his knee's beside me asking forgiveness for what he and his brother had done. He said, "Dear Lord, please help this man and allow him to live, help manage his pain and suffering that we have caused. It's my entire fault, I could have stopped my older brother but, we never meant for anyone to get hurt and as you know Lord…our guns were not even loaded. We only wanted to scare the clerk into giving us his money. Dear God, in the memory of my mother have mercy upon me a sinner, forgive me of my daily sins and the sins I have committed here causing harm to this man. In the name of Jesus Christ I ask for your help."

"Matthew—how terrible, you could have hurt!" LaDonna said.

"Wait darling, there's more," I answered, "to make a long story short, backup officers arrived took the young man in custody just as the ambulance arrived to take Morris to the hospital. A field supervisor told me to ride in the ambulance with my partner and would see that our patrol car was secured and returned to the station. LaDonna, here's the interesting part. On the ride to the hospital Morris was in and out of consciousness, the ambulance driver dispatched our 'ETA', our estimated time of arrival to the hospital, emergency personnel was standing by and everything was put into play for Morris to go straight to surgery. Within minutes after our arrival a member of the hospital surgical team came out to the waiting area where I sat with half a dozen other officers to give us a preliminary evaluation and said, 'Matthew, you can tell your team your partner will be pulling through just fine. He has a strong will and is a just man favored among many.' He turned around and walked back in the surgical area. I settled down to a cup of black coffee that a nurse had provided when yet another surgeon came out to talk to us. 'Officer Anderson', he said, 'I'm Dr. Knoll; I was told the wounded officer is your partner, I just arrived—your friend is being prepped for surgery this very minute and I just wanted your department to know that it looks like a clean wound and can foreseen no major problems. It looks like your friend is a fighter and seems to be in good physical shape, so I'm anticipating approximately three hours of surgical time before we'll know more. We'll take every precaution necessary to help in his recovery but I see little concern that's life threatening.'

I looked at Dr. Knoll and said, "Thank you, your assistant has already been out and gave us his initial prognosis—the same as your."

"What assistant?" Dr. Knoll asked.

"The other male doctor in there with you," I answered.

"Officer—you must be mistaken. I'm the only male surgeon here at the moment. My surgical team is in place but is all female technicians and nurses. Even the anesthesiologist is a nurse practitioner.

"LaDonna, it wasn't until later that mid-morning when I finally knew without question that I had been blessed by a visit from an angelic being. Do you know how I really knew? I was sitting in a waiting room with several other officers, but none of them could recall any such contact from anyone until Dr. Knoll arrived. Then there was the way the angel called me by my first name saying 'Matthew' when delivery his message. LaDonna, he called me by my first name—don't you get it. Dr, Knoll called me by 'Officer Anderson', name tags on police officers uniforms always uses the last name not the first.

It was at that time I realized how sad it was that so few of us actually understanding that in this life 'we never walk alone'. We by ourselves can accomplish nothing—whatever differences we might make is the result of the contributions from those invisible beings, the Holy Spirit and our Guardian Angels walking beside us— whatever masterpiece we have written so to speak is only the result of the prompting and nurturing of our heavenly spirit guides."

"I was so impressed with that young man's plea I made it a point to attend his trial and have stayed in touch with him over the years. He was given four years for his part of the armed robbery, his bother that ran off was given eighteen years. LaDonna, you would never know it—but that young boy is now a minister and operates a half-way house for repeat offenders in the heart of Harlem New York. LaDonna, you have to admit it; God works in mysterious ways beyond ordinary understanding—don't you agree?

"Darling, metaphorically we each have written a book of our own life—the result can be a best seller or simply discarded by our editor deemed not worthy to be read. I often thought that the Bible could be looked at as receiving a 'Letter from God' giving us strength, encouragement and advice. Honey I don't know about you but I love receiving letters from family and friends, don't you? If only man would learn to read his letters life would have a greater meaning."

"Matthew, I've never heard it put so elegantly before. How endearing your choice of words, and how so true," LaDonna said. "I have to condition myself to change my way of thinking and speech. Instead of thanking God for what I thought I needed, I need to thank him for what he knew I needed."

We have all heard that when God closes a door he always opens a window allowing us to have the same opportunity to exercise our free-will and disciple. LaDonna and I were becoming closer with each new passing day, with each new day Abby just seems to drift farther and farther away.

Abby's condition hadn't changed much one way or another. She is just holding on for some reason unknown to me, her time is swiftly approaching; to walk with her Heavenly Father in the garden of paradise. I know that God does not forsake or abandon those who are left behind to struggle with temporal matters. I know that each of us are destined to die and shed this physical body; yet, I wonder and question if I have lived a life good enough, or if my faith is strong enough, to be called a son of God.

The celestial world to come is one that has not been revealed to us by God, this is one of the reasons we each fear death so. No matter how strong we each may believe it is human nature to fear what we can't see or don't understand. But once we overcome that fear there is a promise, a promise of God's absolute love.

The symbolic representations of streets paved with gold, of foundations made of precious stones living in a garden of tranquility are only symbolic. LaDonna, I believe that Heaven is the fulfillment of humanistic dreams, hopes and desires. I think that God's greatest treasure in heaven will be each of us—mankind, having accepted his love freely for all time and eternity.

There have been so many names given for our final resting place where we will spend eternity with God, some call it Heaven, in Hinduism it's called Nirvana other cultures have named it Paradise or Eden, in Greek mythology it is dramatized as being a heavenly place of peaceful splendor where those who are favored by the gods can go when they die known as *Elysian Fields*—but whatever we choose to call it, it is a place of complete bliss holding delights unimaginable to the human mind.

"LaDonna, I know what I am about to tell you is going to seem like a contradiction from what you may believe, it is for most people. When Jesus said in John 14:13 'Let not your heart be troubled; you believe in God, believe also in ME. In My Father's house are many mansions; if it were not so, I would have told you. I go to prepare a place for you. And if I go and prepare a place for you, *I will come again and receive you to MYSELF—that where I am, there you may be also'.*

Since Jesus ascended to heaven after his resurrection, and since God the Father dwells in heaven, we might safely assume that the 'Father's house' of which Jesus spoke is in heaven. Given that Jesus also said, 'I go to prepare a place for you,' we wrongly assume that the 'place' he is preparing is in the Father's house in heaven. This is a misconception. Jesus never said that 'his followers' would go to heaven, on the contrary, Jesus said, 'I will come again and receive you to Myself; that where I am, there you may be also.' The identify text he where he said 'Myself' and 'Where I am you will be also'. It is only through supplemental study that we truly find that Jesus will establish his kingdom right here on this earth, a newly rebuilt earth where we will reign with him by careful interpretation of reading Revelation 3:21, and also Revelation 5:10.

"LaDonna, I also find reassurance in the scripture, '…at death the spirit returns to God who gave it and the body into the grave.'

*"I know that when Abby crosses over she will indeed be with God, and this is the hope that I cherish.* It is impossible to understand the absurd mysteries of this life, why things just happen, it has taken me a long time to come to terms that answers are unimportant—some things are not meant for us to know. Why then does man create conflicts and wars, why did six million Jews die in the holocaust, why do…children die?

It's hard to let children go especially to the grave; it is only by my trust in the Lord that has allowed me find strength in the scriptures, when I am really down and having a 'pity-party' for myself I find by my reading in Psalms particularly Psalms 34:15-22, 'When brokenhearted, I am always close to you'; I somehow able to put my life back on track even if only for a short time.

# Chapter 12: Clemency of Love

God loved us so much even before we were born that he had decided to give his "ONLY" son as a ransom for our sins. LaDonna, when we read John 3:16 we find that God so loved the world, that he gave his only begotten Son, that whoever believes in him should not perish, but have everlasting life.

It's really quite simple; Jesus came to reveal the nature of our Father in Heaven. Jesus said, "If you have seen me, you have seen the Father." God is love; the very nature of the Father is Love, not unlike any human father we may know. The Apostle Paul exclaimed in 2 Corinthians 9:15, that neither the human tongue, nor words in the human vocabulary are able to explain and describe God's gift of love. As mortal man, to even attempt to fathom the love of our heavenly Father love is quite impossible. "That whosoever believeth in him should not perish, but have eternal life" is in many way quite inconceivable, but none-the-less true.

As any loving parent can attest—love is a natural emotion, it—just is. There is no way to actually give explanation. From the time of a child's birth, a parent's love is absolute, it's everything from providing life's necessities to being the band-aid that holds and heals a wound. When a child falls and skins a knee a loving parent as if by supernatural awareness will feel the same pain every bit as much as his child. It doesn't matter if the pain is physical, mental or emotional it is still felt by a loving parent. Long before a relationship with the father can be instilled infants are nurtured principally by the mother because of exposure, especially where breast feeding is involved. A child soon learns that "I am loved simply because I am." This experience of being loved is perceived without restraints and is recognized instinctively as being unconditional.

In my case, nurturing my daughter as both mother and father was without question; the sound of my voice, the tactile touch of my hands and the scent from my cologne or after-shave all conveyed love, warmth and safety to my child. The closer a child feels to their parents the more secure they feel.

With only one exception, our Heavenly Father's love is not unlike that of the love I hold for my daughter, God's love is pure and perfect. God by his very nature is perfect without sin or blemish. As man I wish I could say that. In Matthew 4:48 Jesus said, "Therefore you shall be perfect, just as your Father in heaven is perfect." We as mortal men cannot conceive the infinite yield to God's love, an absolute love without boundaries or limitations.

"LaDonna, let's have a little spiritual banter, a little give and take. I'll bring up a concept and you address it the best way you can. Tell me what you think, share with me what you believe—actually what I am trying to do is find understanding by logically looking at a viewpoint from a mortal man's point of view. First God is flawless—correct."

"Yes Matthew, I believe that God is flawless and perfect in every way imaginable," LaDonna said.

"Okay then," I said, "knowing that God is perfection and adding the concept that mankind was created in his image along with the idea that God is compassionate—do you think that God feels human anguish and suffering?"

"Matthew—what you said it does make sense that since God is compassionate and his love is endless, then it only stands to reason that he must feel what we may be feeling. I mean, how could he understand the pain we may be feeling if he himself never felt the same pain," LaDonna said.

"Good point, LaDonna," I said, "let me add something else. I'm sure we'll agree that the Holy Trinity of the Father, the Son, and the Holy Spirit are ONE entity. Well—if the Father is also the Son and the Son is also the Father and we know based on scripture that Christ Jesus wept, that goes to say that God cries also?"

"Darling," LaDonna said, "it only stands to reason that since Jesus was born of a woman just like us, lived in this same world that we live in, experienced every emotion that every man from the beginning of time had ever known, prevailed against the temptations of Satan and understands our very nature of life—of pain, suffering and anguish, then I can't help but think that God cannot help but feel remorse for our sins and actually cries tears in the same way that we do. Matthew, I have always imagined God the Father as a caring, loving benevolent being. Since I have never seen God I can only relate to him as I have pictured him in my mind. God is a rather large man some six feet in height with hair of solid white. Actually in fact he looks much like any other man you may pass on the street with the exception that he has a glow about himself. When I pray this is the image I recall when thinking of my Heavenly Father."

"So, LaDonna, you do believe God the Father feels the pain of mankind. Well, I agree with you, partly," I said. "I don't think God as the man Jesus was crying because he identified with the pain—but rather he cried because he felt the pain himself. I believe he cried because he actually felt the pain and anguish as any man would do. God's love is so profound and encompassing he can't help but hurt when we do.

"When Jesus died for our sins on the cross, he died for the past, present and future sins of all mankind. Every sin ever committed or ever will be committed was wiped-clean and forgiven but only if we have a repentant heart and contrite spirit. LaDonna, can you imagine—I know I can't even begin to comprehend the weight on Jesus's shoulders carrying the burden of sin for the world. But he did! Sins of sadness and despair, sins of hopelessness anger and grief, sins of betrayal and even blasphemy. Sins which had committed by every kind of criminal from the arsonist to the rapist, from the drug peddler to kidnappers. Sins from those who were attempting to be righteous but fell short, for it is written—all men sin.

Abby maintained her dignity until the very end by showing that death in itself was just the beginning of life. She also showed me that death need not be a time for sorrow.

On the early morning hours of her thirteenth birthday she gave up her spirit and became reunited with her Father in Heaven. Before doing so she awoke from her coma, to give to me the greatest *gift* I have ever known. It was shortly after midnight when she opened her eye's and called for me.

LaDonna and I both huddled over the head of her bed, crying with tears of joy and relief. As I started to speak, Abby reached up and placed her fingertips on my lips and said,

"Daddy—LaDonna, I want you to know that I love you both, my time has come but before I go remember what you have taught me— don't look upon my death with sorrow, but as a sacred and blessed experience of life yet to come. It's true, Daddy, there are angel's who look after us. They not only guide and direct our lives, but protect us from the evils of darkness. Remember, by your teachings it was you who taught me that the Bible says that we need to be watchful for we may be entertaining Angel's unaware. It's all true! Sometimes it's a feeling that we can't describe a little prod or nudge, or even something as simple as a soft soothing sound or a scent of freshly cut flowers, it's different for each of us—but they are everywhere watching, protecting and providing for our well being.

"Daddy, angels even speak to us if only we would listen for their words of comfort and guidance. The love of God is never-ending. Daddy, true spiritual growth can only begin once we have shed our mortal bodies. Please, be happy for me, the angel's of death are nothing to fear; for they and they alone hold the keys to spiritual consciousness. Daddy, I love you—God's symbolic tears convey the image of a father's love, a love like yours.

With these few words, Abby took her last breath here on earth and died a few minutes after midnight. Today would have been the anniversary of her birth, finally becoming a teenager. LaDonna and I both just stood there, unable to speak or react to the lost of our darling child, yet knowing she was at peace with the heavenly host.

Today, my precious daughter Abby gave me a gift...a gift of *spiritual awareness that can only come from our Father in Heaven.*

Abby's funeral service was plain and unadorned, modest by some Christian standards yet priceless to her Jewish heritage, she was laid to rest in our family mausoleum.

As for me I now have a new awareness of eternal life.

LaDonna and I were married the following month surrounded by our dear friends at the hospice. We thought it only befitting that the ceremony takes place in the courtyard looking up to Abby's room, where our lives actually began.

I am confident that The Heavenly Host rejoiced with tears of gladness on the day of Abby's death to welcome her to her new home, for we know the love of God instinctively and rely upon his love for now and all eternity.

Today, I do not mourn my daughters' death but celebrate her release from this mortal life knowing that God is love, and who-so-ever lives in love lives in God. How great is the love the Father has lavished on us, that we should be called his children, because my friends…that's what we are—His Children!

Lastly, consider for a moment what parent hasn't shed a tear or cried for their child from time to time, now I ask you…can God the Father do any less?